PROMOTING LOCAL CURRENCY SUSTAINABLE FINANCE IN ASEAN+3

JUNE 2022

ADB

ASIAN DEVELOPMENT BANK

© 2022 Asian Development Bank
6 ADB Avenue, Mandaluyong City, 1550 Metro Manila, Philippines
Tel +63 2 8632 4444; Fax +63 2 8636 2444
www.adb.org

Some rights reserved. Published in 2022.

ISBN 978-92-9269-576-7 (print); 978-92-9269-577-4 (electronic); 978-92-9269-578-1 (ebook)
Publication Stock No. TCS220251-2
DOI: http://dx.doi.org/10.22617/TCS220251-2

Note:
In this publication, "$" refers to United States dollars.
ADB recognizes "China" as the People's Republic of China; "Hong Kong" as Hong Kong, China; "Korea" as the Republic of Korea; "Macao" as Macau, China; "Siam" as Thailand; "Vietnam" as Viet Nam; and "Saigon" as Ho Chi Minh City.

Cover design by Kookie Trivino.

Printed on recycled paper

Contents

Tables, Figures, and Boxes

Boxes

Foreword

The Asian Development Bank (ADB) is collaborating closely with the Association of Southeast Asian Nations (ASEAN), the People's Republic of China (PRC), Japan, and the Republic of Korea—collectively known as ASEAN+3—to promote the development of local currency bond markets and regional bond market integration through the Asian Bond Markets Initiative (ABMI). ABMI was established in 2002 to bolster the region's financial system's resilience by developing local currency bond markets as an alternative to foreign currency short-term bank loans for long-term investment financing.

This study was conducted under ABMI with generous financial support from the Government of the PRC through the PRC Poverty Reduction and Regional Cooperation Fund.

Since the publication of *Promoting Green Local Currency Bonds for Infrastructure Development in ASEAN+3* in 2018, the ASEAN+3 region's sustainable finance landscape has shifted dramatically. Not only has the region seen rapid growth in green bond issuance, but also in social and sustainability bond issuance and more innovative instruments such as green loans and sustainability-linked bonds. Meanwhile, several ASEAN+3 governments have implemented regulatory and incentive measures to promote the development of sustainable finance markets in their respective jurisdictions.

Significant developments were also observed in the ASEAN region following the introduction of ASEAN green, social, and sustainability bond standards by the ASEAN Capital Markets Forum in 2018. Notably, in 2020, ASEAN central banks published the *Roles of ASEAN Central Banks in Managing Climate and Environment-Related Risks*. That same year, the ASEAN Capital Markets Forum published the *Roadmap for ASEAN Sustainable Capital Markets*. And most recently, the ASEAN Taxonomy Board launched the *ASEAN Taxonomy for Sustainable Finance (Version 1)*, a significant step toward meeting Paris Agreement commitments by establishing a common language for financing sustainable economic activities. As climate change and social issues transcend national boundaries, cross-border collaboration and integration can undoubtedly play a critical role in the region's collective response to these issues.

This report, prepared by the Asian Development Bank (ADB) in collaboration with the Climate Bonds Initiative, analyzes the sustainable bond market's recent growth and current state; discusses policies and strategies for promoting local currency sustainable finance in the ASEAN+3 region; and provides recommendations for the regional market's development, particularly among emerging economies.

Under the guidance of ABMI, ADB will continue to play a critical role in supporting ASEAN+3 economies to develop sustainable finance markets that will contribute to the region meeting Paris Agreement targets.

Albert Francis Park
Chief Economist and Director General
Economic Research and Regional Cooperation Department
Asian Development Bank

Acknowledgments

This report was jointly prepared by staff of the Asian Development Bank (ADB) and Climate Bonds Initiative.

A team of ADB staff—led by Kosintr Puongsophol, financial sector specialist, Economic Research and Regional Cooperation Department (ERCD), Asian Development Bank and comprising Richard Supangan, Oth Marulou Gagni, Alita Lestor, and Rob Fowler, all of ERCD—coordinated the overall production of this report under the guidance of Satoru Yamadera, advisor, ERCD.

A team of Climate Bonds Initiative staff, led by Daniel McGree and with significant contributions from Phi Thi Minh Nguyet and Matthew MacGeoch, led the drafting and preparation of this report.

The authors wish to express their heartfelt gratitude to ASEAN+3 officials for their contributions and guidance throughout the production process. The authors would also like to thank Shu Tian, Naeeda Crishna Morgado, Marina Lopez Andrich, and Karthik Iyer for their inputs. Kevin Donahue provided editorial assistance, and the cover design by Kookie Trivino and layout were completed by Edith Creus.

Abbreviations

ABMI	Asian Bond Markets Initiative
ACGF	ASEAN Catalytic Green Finance Facility
ACMF	ASEAN Capital Markets Forum
ADB	Asian Development Bank
AIF	ASEAN Infrastructure Fund
ASEAN	Association of Southeast Asian Nations
ASEAN+3	ASEAN plus the People's Republic of China, Japan, and the Republic of Korea
bps	basis points
BRL	Brazilian real
BSP	Bangko Sentral ng Pilipinas (Philippines)
CBIRC	China Banking and Insurance Regulatory Commission
CCPT	Climate Change and Principle-Based Taxonomy
CNY	Chinese yuan
COVID-19	coronavirus disease
CSRC	China Securities Regulatory Commission
EDL-Gen	EDL Generation Public Company
ENCON	Energy Conservation Promotion
ESG	environmental, social, and governance
ETS	emissions trading scheme
EUR	euro
FSA	Financial Services Agency (Japan)
FSC	Financial Services Commission (Republic of Korea)
GBP	Green Bond Principles
GBP	UK pound sterling
GDP	gross domestic product
GHG	greenhouse gas
GSS	green, sustainable, and social
GTFS	Green Technology Financing Scheme (Malaysia)
H1	first half
HKD	Hong Kong dollar
HKMA	Hong Kong Monetary Authority

ICMA	International Capital Market Association
IDX	PT Bursa Efek Indonesia
JPY	Japanese yen
KPEI	PT Kliring Penjaminan Efek Indonesia
KPI	key performance indicator
KRW	Korean won
KSEI	PT Kustodian Sentral Efek Indonesia
LCY	local currency
LGFA	local government funding agency
MAS	Monetary Authority of Singapore
METI	Ministry of Economy, Trade and Industry (Japan)
MYR	Malaysian ringgit
NAFMII	National Association of Financial Market Institutional Investors
NDRC	National Development and Reform Commission (PRC)
OJK	Financial Services Authority (Indonesia)
PBOC	People's Bank of China
PRC	People's Republic of China
Q	quarter
SBP	Social Bond Principles
SCM	Securities Commission Malaysia
SDGs	Sustainable Development Goals
SEC Thailand	Securities and Exchange Commission, Thailand
SERC	Securities and Exchange Regulator of Cambodia
SET	Stock Exchange of Thailand
SGD	Singapore dollar
SGX	Singapore Exchange
SLB	sustainability-linked bond
SLL	sustainability-linked loan
SMEs	small and medium-sized enterprises
SRI	sustainable responsible investment
TA	technical assistance
TCFD	Taskforce on Climate-Related Financial Disclosures (Japan)
ThaiBMA	Thai Bond Market Association
THB	Thailand baht
UN	United Nations
UOP	use-of-proceeds
USD	United States dollar
VND	Vietnamese dong

Key Highlights

Sustainable finance serves a critical role in channeling private investment toward the transition to a low-carbon, climate-resilient, and inclusive economy. The sustainable debt market has historically been dominated by green bonds, but the pandemic has catalyzed the next generation of social and sustainability-labeled instruments to fund a broader range of environmental and social benefits.

The ASEAN+3 region has seen rapid growth not only in green bond issuance but also in the issuance of social and sustainability bonds.* This is reflected in the diverse set of trends toward performance-linked instruments and transition bonds. Growth in the green, sustainable, and social (GSS) debt market was buoyed in 2020 and the first 3 quarters of 2021 by social bonds being issued as an immediate response to the impacts of the coronavirus disease (COVID-19) pandemic, as well as by increased sustainability bond issuance in the first half of 2021 (Figure H1).

Figure H1: ASEAN+3 Total Sustainable Bond Issuance

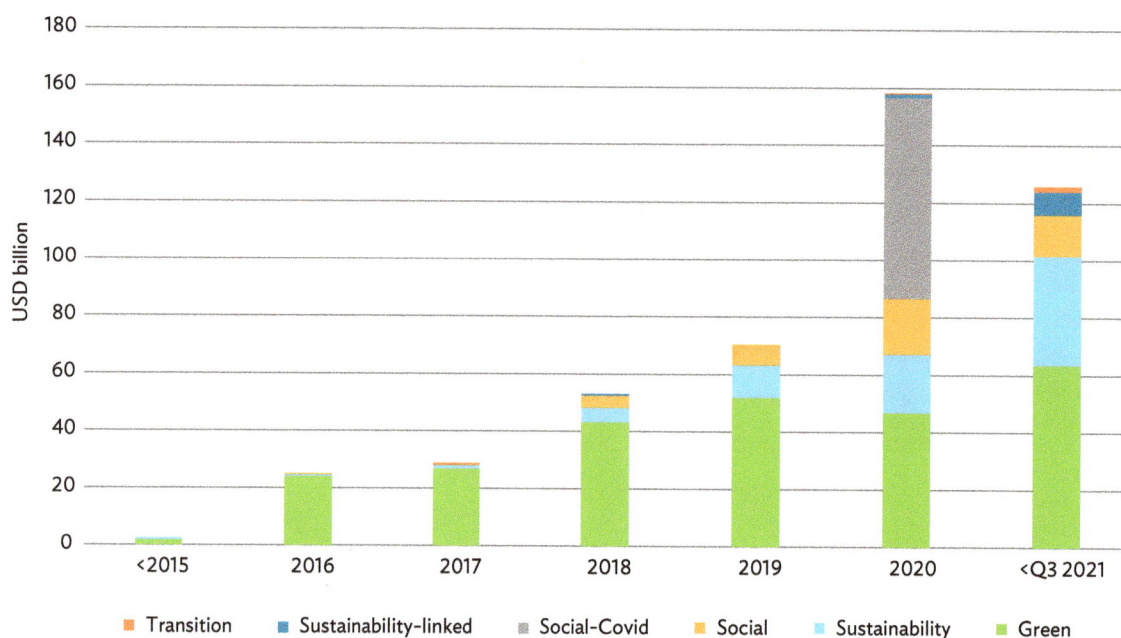

Legend: Transition ▪ Sustainability-linked ▪ Social-Covid ▪ Social ▪ Sustainability ▪ Green

ASEAN+3 = Association of Southeast Asian Nations plus the People's Republic of China (PRC), Japan, and the Republic of Korea; COVID-19 = coronavirus disease; USD = United States dollar.
Source: Climate Bonds Initiative.

---

* ASEAN+3 comprises members of the Association of Southeast Asian Nations (ASEAN) plus the People's Republic of China, Japan, and the Republic of Korea.

At the end of the third quarter of 2021, the cumulative sustainable debt market in ASEAN+3 had reached a size of USD449 billion. The region's larger economies have driven regional growth, with the People's Republic of China (PRC); Hong Kong, China; and Japan responsible for 61.4% of that volume. Outside these larger economies, important issuances have come to market including Thailand's THB-denominated sovereign sustainability bond, Malaysia's USD-denominated sovereign sustainability *sukuk* (the world's first such bond), Indonesia' inaugural Sustainable Development Goal bond, and Singapore's National Environment Agency's first green bond. The spike in local currency (LCY) issuance as a share of total issuance during the review period can generally be attributed to the impact of large-scale, social-COVID-19 issuances from the PRC, Japan, Malaysia, Singapore, and Thailand (Figure H2).

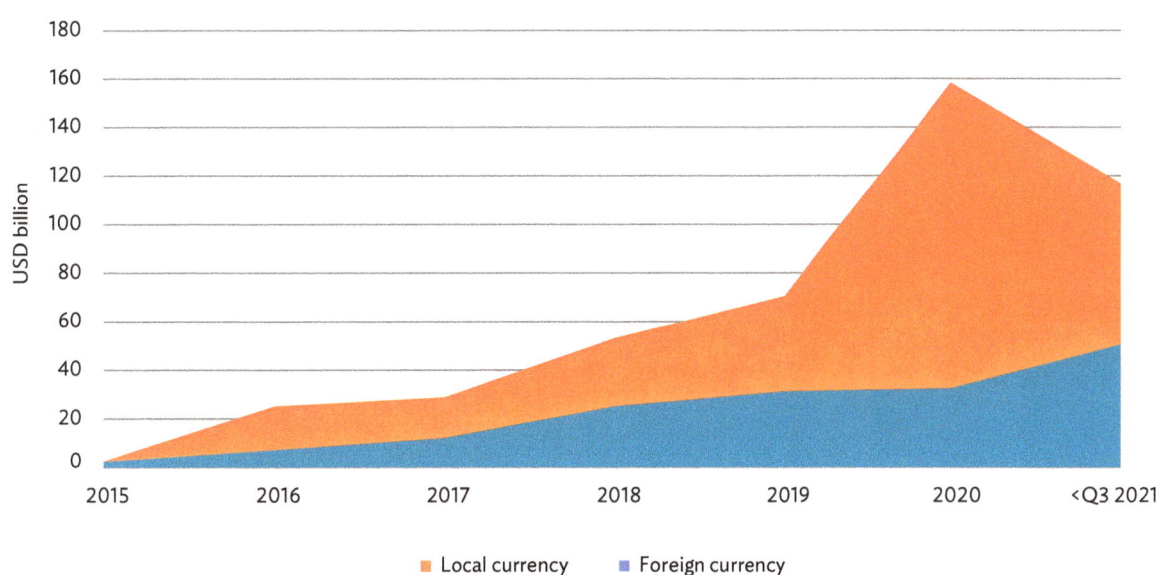

Figure H2: ASEAN+3 Share of Local Currency in Sustainable Debt Issuances

ASEAN+3 = Association of Southeast Asian Nations plus the People's Republic of China (PRC), Japan, and the Republic of Korea, USD = United States dollar.
Source: Climate Bonds Initiative.

While supply has increased, demand for GSS bonds is growing from a variety of sources. Greater investor understanding of climate risk, new fund launches, and a broadening market presence have all stimulated demand. Sustainable finance instruments can encourage further investment across ASEAN+3 economies when underpinned by GSS finance frameworks and clear issuance processes. The creation of transparent sustainable financing approaches and instruments is fundamental to incentivizing investment as well as the transition to more sustainable practices.

The region's LCY bond markets can further support the development of the sustainable bond segment in the region. Less than half of ASEAN+3 economies—the PRC, Japan, Malaysia, Singapore, and Thailand— account for a majority of the region's LCY sustainable debt issuance. Thailand stands out as having the largest share of LCY bonds among its total sustainable debt, with 98.5% of its sustainable det issuance, worth the equivalent of USD10.6 billion, denominated in Thai baht (Figure H3). On the other hand, Hong Kong, China; Indonesia; the Republic of Korea; the Philippines; and Viet Nam issued a majority of their sustainable debt in foreign currencies. Viet Nam stands out as having the largest share of its sustainable debt denominated in foreign currencies at 96.1% (the equivalent of USD656.8 million). Indonesia has 94.6% of its debt denominated in foreign currencies, while the Philippines has a more balanced share of 53.9%.

Figure H3: Sustainable Bond Issuance in ASEAN+3 Economies—Local Currency versus Foreign Currency

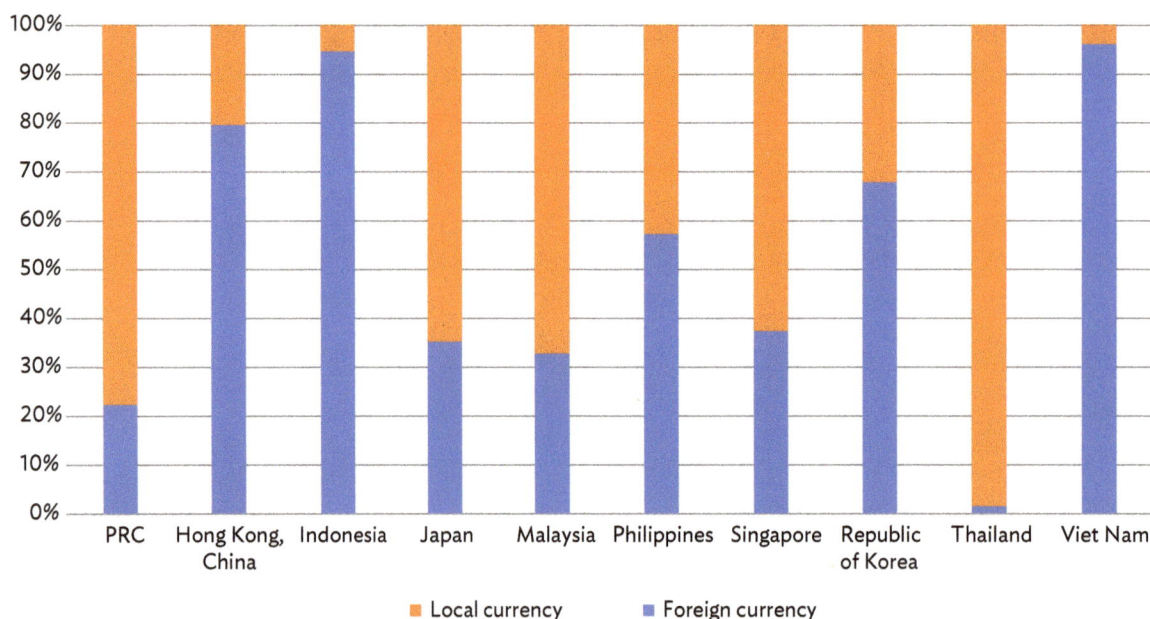

ASEAN+3 = Association of Southeast Asian Nations plus the People's Republic of China (PRC), Japan, and the Republic of Korea.
Note: Data reflects cumulative issuance through the end of September 2021.
Source: Climate Bonds Initiative.

Several domestic and regional policies and actions reflect the continuing progress being made to promote LCY sustainable finance. For instance, the People's Bank of China published a *Green Bond Endorsed Projects Catalogue*. Within the ASEAN region, the *ASEAN Taxonomy for Sustainable Finance (Version 1)* is designed to be interoperable with other regional and international taxonomies, and it will serve as a common building block that enables an orderly transition and fosters sustainable finance adoption by all ASEAN member states.

The ASEAN+3 market is not homogeneous, and the stage of market development varies across economies. To deliver on international climate and sustainability commitments, billions of dollars' worth of public and private capital is needed for new public works projects in renewable energy, low-carbon transport, sustainable water management, and sustainable waste management. To achieve this, the following recommendations are proposed for the region to address bottlenecks to attracting additional investment in green financing opportunities.

Supply Side

1. **Sovereign GSS bond issuance.** Emerging market sovereign issuance can channel sustainable capital flows where they are most needed.

2. **Unlabeled (climate-aligned) universe.** These are investment opportunities that are not explicitly labeled as "green" by the issuer but still finance climate-aligned assets and activities.

3. **Advisory services for issuers.** Both public- and private-sector advisory services can (i) support new issuers with limited sustainable finance experience in determining the types of projects and assets that qualify as sustainable finance, and (ii) address misperceptions that GSS bonds carry considerably higher

costs. These services could be institutionalized through collaboration between the government and a development partner or via a government agency that makes such services accessible.

4. **Grant schemes.** Regulators and central banks can use grants to encourage sustainable finance flows.

5. **Green project pipelines.** The growth of green infrastructure pipelines and associated green finance (including the green bond market) can be aided by policy and institutional changes. International multilateral development agencies play a key role in blended finance, providing capital that mobilizes green and sustainable projects.

Demand Side

1. **Expand the investor base.** Regional bond market authorities can capitalize on increasing demand from institutional investors seeking sustainable investment opportunities.

2. **Central banks can help "build back better."** The post-pandemic recovery toolkit can be used by central banks to protect ASEAN+3 member states from future systemic risks—particularly climate-related risks.

3. **GSS bond exchange-traded funds and indices.** Efforts should be made to promote increased investor awareness of and participation in sustainable bond markets.

Ecosystem

1. **Mandates from government and regulators.** Securities regulators, capital market authorities, and/or central banks should provide support mechanisms to encourage green, social, and sustainability bond issuance.

2. **GSS and sustainable finance platforms.** It would be beneficial for information on green assets and projects to be centralized in an easy-to-access portal or platform that is available in multiple languages.

1 Introduction

Background

A fundamental shift in the way capital is being allocated within global markets is currently taking place. The triple threats of climate change, environmental degradation, and social inequalities—together with the impacts of the coronavirus disease (COVID-19)—highlight the need for new financing mechanisms to ensure a sustainable future.[1] The awareness of these threats by the financial sector has led to the development of a sustainable finance market to directly address these challenges at scale.

Since the first green bonds were issued by the European Investment Bank and the World Bank in 2007, the sustainable debt market has grown exponentially. The market now involves debt issued by over 67 economies and multiple supranational institutions, and it incorporates a variety of public and private sector participants. The global green bond market reached a milestone of USD1.0 trillion in issuance in December 2020, representing an estimated growth rate of 95% per annum.

The sustainable debt market has historically been dominated by green bonds, but the pandemic has catalyzed the next generation of social- and sustainability-labeled instruments to fund a broader range of environmental and social benefits. The publication of the Sustainability Bond Guidelines by the International Capital Market Association (ICMA) in June 2018 paved the way for combining the green project categories of the Green Bond Principles (GBP) and the social categories of the Social Bond Principles (SBP).

The ASEAN+3 region—which comprises the bonds markets of the 10 members of the Association of Southeast Asian Nations (ASEAN) plus the People's Republic of China (PRC), Japan, and the Republic of Korea—has seen rapid growth not only in green bond issuance but also in the social and sustainability bond markets. This is reflected in the diverse set of trends toward performance-linked instruments and transition bonds.

This report provides a regional update on the green, social, sustainable, sustainability-linked, and transition bond market, with a particular focus on local currency (LCY) sustainable bond markets in ASEAN+3. The first section defines the financial instruments that constitute the global climate bond market. The second section gives a snapshot of the current state of the global green, sustainable, and social (GSS) market, together with a closer look at the ASEAN+3 region. The third section outlines recent regional and national initiatives, approaches, and policy developments to promote local currency (LCY) sustainable finance. The fourth section highlights green investment opportunities in ASEAN+3. This report concludes with recommendations and possible next steps for ASEAN+3 to further advance sustainable LCY bond market development in the region. Unless otherwise stated, all data in this report come from the Green Bond Database of the Climate Bonds Initiative (Climate Bonds).

---

[1]   Frederic Asseline and Bradley Hiller. 2021. *Green, Social, and Sustainability Bonds: Market Overview and ADB's Participation*. Manila: ADB.

Table 1: Cumulative Thematic Bond Issuances in ASEAN+3 through Q3 2021
(USD billion)

	Green	Sustainability	Social	Social-COVID-19	Sustainability-Linked	Transition	Total
PRC	165.68	6.50	1.10	68.01	5.45	0.28	**247.02**
Hong Kong, China	12.69	1.11	0.83		1.05	1.90	**17.58**
Indonesia	6.29	0.55	0.50		0.61		**7.94**
Japan	29.85	21.94	16.64	0.13	0.98	0.18	**69.72**
Malaysia	1.44	3.08					**4.52**
Philippines	3.45	2.25		0.44			**6.14**
Singapore	19.63	1.58	0.05		1.25	0.31	**22.82**
Republic of Korea	17.27	23.29	26.44	1.50			**68.50**
Thailand	2.17	8.14	0.29		0.15		**10.76**
Viet Nam	0.68						**0.68**
Total	**259.15**	**68.44**	**45.86**	**70.09**	**9.48**	**2.67**	**455.68**

ASEAN+3 = Association of Southeast Asian Nations (ASEAN), the People's Republic of China (PRC), Japan and the Republic of Korea; COVID-19 = coronavirus disease; USD = United States dollar.
Source: Climate Bonds Initiative.

Financial Instruments Covered in This Study

Sustainable debt instruments are defined as instruments that have a label and directly finance sustainable projects or assets in the form of use-of-proceeds (UOP) bonds and labeled loans. The three GSS debt themes are based on the projects, assets, and activities financed.

Green Bonds

A green bond is commonly defined as a labeled fixed-income instrument where proceeds are specifically allocated for climate or other environmental projects. These are targeted typically (but not limited) to projects tackling energy efficiency, pollution prevention, sustainable agriculture, fishery and forestry management, protection of aquatic and terrestrial ecosystems, clean transportation, clean water, and sustainable water management, among others.

While there is no universally accepted definition of what constitutes an eligible project for funding with green bond proceeds, Climate Bonds and this report employ the Climate Bonds Taxonomy, which includes eight UOP categories: (i) energy, (ii) buildings, (iii) transportation, (iv) water, (v) waste, (vi) land use, (vii) industry, and (viii) information and communication technology (ICT). The taxonomy is based on the Climate Bonds Standard, which is made up of sector criteria developed with the help of international scientists and industry experts. Under the Climate Bonds Standard Version 3.0, issuers can appoint an approved verifier to certify their green debt instruments. The verifier certifies that the UOP complies with the goal of keeping global warming below 2°C.

Every deal with a green label variant has been screened for inclusion in the relevant database. The Green Bond Database Methodology of Climate Bonds specifies a set of process rules for screening:[2]

- deals must carry a variant of the green label, and
- all net proceeds must verifiably (based on public disclosure) meet Climate Bonds' green definitions based on the Climate Bonds Taxonomy.[3]

The green bond database only include bonds with 100% of proceeds dedicated to green assets and projects that are aligned with the Climate Bonds Taxonomy. A bond may be excluded if there is insufficient information on allocations.

Social and Sustainability Bonds

Drawing on existing market references and extensive research, the inclusion of social and sustainability bonds provides broad guidance on eligible sectors (and subsectors) that can be funded with social and sustainability bonds. Although work on a social taxonomy is underway in the European Union and elsewhere, neither a comprehensive taxonomy nor an equivalent classification and screening system for debt instruments aiming to achieve positive social or sustainable outcomes has yet been developed.[4] As a result, the UOP of social and sustainability bonds is not compared to performance benchmarks. They are, however, classified according to their labels and are divided into the following categories:

- **Social.** The label is exclusively applied to financing new and existing projects with positive social outcomes such as education, access to essential services, employment generation, and affordable housing.
- **Sustainability.** The label is exclusively applied to financing or refinancing a combination of both green and social projects. The green project categories in these instruments are screened by Climate Bonds' Green Bond Database Methodology.[5]

Transition Bonds

Transition finance refers to instruments that are used to fund activities that are not low- or zero-emission, but that play a short- or long-term role in decarbonizing an activity or assisting an issuer in transitioning to compliance with the Paris Agreement. As a result, the transition label allows a wider range of sectors and activities to be included in the universe of sustainable finance.

Transition bonds are currently derived primarily from polluting and difficult-to-abate industries. They do not fit any of the existing definitions of green bonds, but they are an essential part of the net-zero transition. Economic sectors include extractive industries such as mining, materials such as steel and cement, and other industries such as aviation. Specific key performance indicators (KPIs) and screening indicators for transition activities have already begun to be developed. Climate Bonds began with the 2020 release of a white paper, *Financing Credible Transitions,* which was followed by the launch of a discussion paper, *Transition Finance for Transforming Companies* in September 2021. This is complemented by the process guidelines in the ICMA's *Climate Transition Finance Handbook* released in December 2020.

---

[2]   Climate Bonds Initiative. 2020. *Green Bond Database Methodology.* London.
[3]   Climate Bonds Initiative.2020. *Climate Bonds Taxonomy.* London.
[4]   European Commission. EU taxonomy for sustainable activities. https://ec.europa.eu/info/business-economy-euro/banking-and-finance/sustainable-finance/eu-taxonomy-sustainable-activities_en.
[5]   For more information on methodology and segmentation, please refer to Appendix 2.

Sustainability-Linked Bonds

Performance- or KPI-linked debt instruments, more commonly known as sustainability-linked bonds (SLBs) or sustainability-linked loans (SLLs), raise general-purpose finance and involve financial penalties if predefined, time-bound sustainability performance targets (e.g., greenhouse gas [GHG] or carbon dioxide emission reductions) are not met (Box 1).[6] These penalties often either involve one or more of the following:

- coupon step-ups: an increase in the cost or amount of debt to be repaid (often from 10 to 75 basis points [bps]);
- premium payment: a self-imposed fine to be paid into an environmental, social, and governance (ESG) specific account; and
- offset purchase obligation: the mandatory purchase of carbon offsets (often used alongside one of the above penalties).

SLBs and SLLs are tied to meeting one or more predefined, time-bound KPIs related to broader sustainability performance targets at the entity level, rather than financing a specific pool of assets and projects. In principle, the issuer has few restrictions on how the funds raised are spent, as long as the performance improvements are verifiable and consistent progress is made over time.

Box 1: Other Relevant Instruments under Development Globally

The flexibility of performance-linked instruments allows them to be used in conjunction with existing sustainable finance instruments, as well as the creation of new derivative instruments that have come to market recently. Combinations with existing sustainable finance instruments include green sustainability-linked bonds, transition SLBs, and (potentially) social SLBs. These structures include the use-of-proceeds requirements of a green, social, sustainability, or transition bond, while also attaching the financial mechanisms that characterize SLBs.

The flexibility also allows for the issuance of other more niche performance-linked instruments, such as a sustainability-linked enhanced equipment trust certificate, which is a form of bond that allows the issuer to purchase an asset using the funds that are predominately used by the aviation and shipping industries for tax benefits in the United States. It also allows for the recent creation of sustainability-relinked bonds, a form of derivative that ties the financial mechanism of the bond to the financial mechanism of the underlying SLBs or sustainability-linked loans (SLLs). This form of instrument can help to bring transparency to the otherwise opaque market of SLLs, where there is rarely any public disclosure of the key performance indicators or financial mechanisms that allow it to join the sustainable finance universe.

Source: Climate Bonds Initiative.

SLBs and SLLs are an important part of the sustainable finance landscape, especially for enabling entity-level transitions. The Climate Bonds' *Transition Principles* and the associated *Financing Credible Transitions* iterate guidance on transition definitions and appropriate levels of ambition, whereas the ICMA's *Sustainability-Linked Bond Principles* provide useful preliminary guidance on the issuance process.[7]

---

[6]   Excerpt from Climate Bonds Initiative. 2021. *Post Issuance Reporting in the Green Bond Market.* https://www.climatebonds.net/resources/reports/post-issuance-reporting-green-bond-market-2021.
[7]   ICMA. 2020. *Sustainability-Linked Bond Principles.* Zurich.

Green Loans

Green loans are any type of loan used to finance or refinance projects, assets, or activities that benefit the environment. Green loans are based on UOP, with borrowing proceeds earmarked for eligible green assets in a transparent manner. Green loans should be structured in accordance with the Green Loan Principles, the Climate Bonds Standard (to the extent that criteria are available), and several country-specific guidelines widely used in the sustainable finance market in the form of KPIs or performance-linked instruments.

Carbon-Neutral Bonds

A carbon-neutral bond is a debt-financing instrument that raises funds exclusively for green projects that reduce carbon emissions. Its primary objective is to direct funds to green, low-carbon, and cyclical sectors, as well as to assist markets and countries in achieving carbon-neutrality objectives. These were first defined by the PRC's National Association of Financial Market Institutional Investors (NAFMII) in March 2021.

Blue Bonds

Issuers may use the blue label if the funds are primarily used to support marine conservation and sustainable use of marine resources. Issuers must disclose information about the impact of relevant projects on the marine environment, the marine economy, and any other benefits to the climate.

While it is important to note that not all blue bonds meet the green requirements (e.g., fisheries enforcement may require the use of fossil fuels). For this study, carbon-neutral bonds and blue bonds are grouped as a subcategory of green bonds.

Poverty Alleviation Bonds

Poverty alleviation bonds, which have been introduced in the PRC, are closely related to the goal of poverty eradication. "No Poverty" is the first of the 17 United Nations (UN) Sustainable Development Goals (SDGs) and is an important component of sustainable development globally.

Poverty alleviation bonds have been used by government-backed entities, local governments, and corporate issuers to finance poverty alleviation and relocation. Issuance-defining bodies include the People's Bank of China, the Shanghai Stock Exchange, and the Shenzhen Stock Exchange.

Rural Revitalization Bonds

Rural revitalization bonds, which have been introduced in the PRC, refer to publicly or non-publicly listed bonds that raise funds for consolidating the results of poverty eradication, promoting the development of poverty-eradicated areas, and carrying out comprehensive rural revitalization. Green rural revitalization bonds are also on the rise since NAFMII clarified that rural revitalization bonds can be used in conjunction with other types of debt financing instruments.

For this study, poverty alleviation bonds and rural revitalization bonds are grouped as a subcategory of social bonds, and green rural revitalization bonds are grouped as a subcategory of green bonds.

Global Trends in Sustainable Finance

By the end of the third quarter (Q3) of 2021, the global sustainable debt market had recorded cumulative issuance of USD2.5 trillion, with almost 10,000 debt instruments having been issued bearing GSS, SLB, or transition bond labels since 2006. The annual issuance volume of the sustainable debt market was well on its way to USD1.0 trillion in 2021, having reached USD782.5 billion by the end of September.[8] This amount represented 55.0% year-on-year growth from the equivalent period in 2020 (USD503.2 billion). It also set the market on track to reach a record-high in 2021, having already surpassed the 2020 total of USD735.0 billion in sustainable debt issuance (Figure 1).

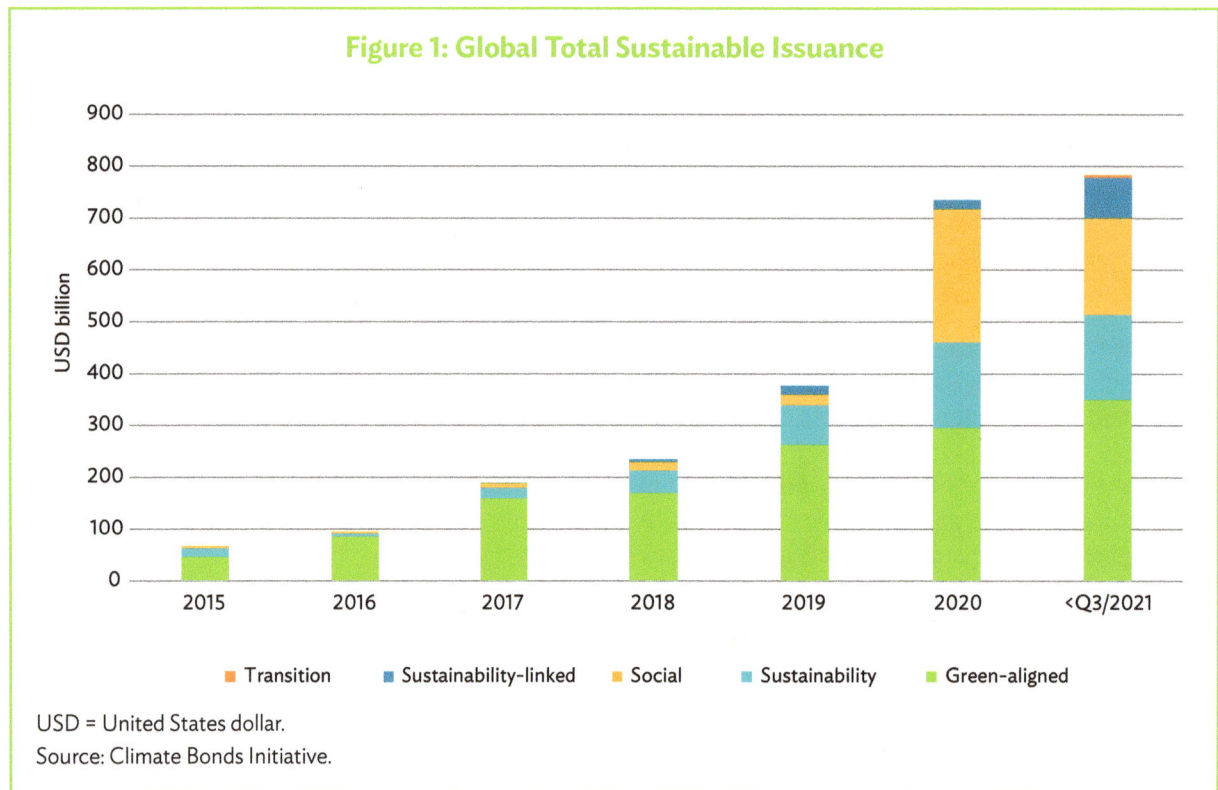

Figure 1: Global Total Sustainable Issuance

USD = United States dollar.
Source: Climate Bonds Initiative.

While green continued to be the dominant theme and the largest source of outright capital in 2021, social and sustainability themes gained significant traction. Due to the need to finance COVID-19 response measures, the majority of non-green issuance in the first half (H1) of 2020 financed pandemic-related investments, before such issuance volume slowed in 2021 despite the pandemic's continued economic impact.

---

8   Climate Bonds Initiative. Sustainable Debt Summary Q3 2021. https://www.climatebonds.net/resources/reports/sustainable-debt-summary-q3-2021.

After a record year in 2020, social and sustainability bond issuance moderated during the first 3 quarters of 2021. This was in part due to the slowdown in the European Union's (EU) Support to Mitigate Unemployment Risk in an Emergency (SURE) social bond issuance—a special program launched to combat the immediate economic repercussions of the pandemic—which amounted to USD38.7 billion in Q1 2021, USD17.3 billion in Q2 2021, and zero new issuance in Q3 2021.

Table 2: Global Cumulative Green, Social, and Sustainability Issuance, Q1 2016–Q3 2021

	Green	Sustainability	Social	Transition	Sustainability-Linked
Total size of the market	**USD1.36 trillion**	**USD492.5 billion**	**USD498.1 billion**	**USD9.95 billion**	**USD112.4 billion**
Number of issuers	1,428	178	601	16	146
Number of instruments	7,716	885	1,230	30	215
Number of countries	71	30	36	11	32
Number of currencies	42	33	25	6	15

Q = quarter, USD = United States dollar.
Source: Climate Bonds Initiative.

New product launches have been facilitated by changing market conditions. The rapid adoption of SLBs was due to a growing number of entities, particularly corporations, seeking access to long-term financing that is not tied to a specific pool of projects, assets, or expenditures. Indeed, the SLB market segment exponentially soared in size in H1 2021, with issuance totaling USD32.9 billion, accounting for 6% of total labeled debt issuance of USD496.1 billion. In H1 2020, on the other hand, no SLBs were issued. In Q3 2021, SLB issuance totaled USD37.0 billion, accounting for 16.8% of the total universe of sustainable debt.

The transition bond market is still in its nascent stage: only 14 transition bonds worth USD5.0 billion were issued in the first 9 months of 2021, out of a total of 30 instruments (USD9.9 billion). All of the bonds issued in Q3 2021 originated in the shipping sector, which Climate Bonds believes is well-positioned to leverage transition financing to achieve rapid decarbonization (Table 2).

Volumes by Currency

The labeled bond market is dominated by hard currency issuance. Through the end of Q3 2021, 84.9% of sustainable bond issuance was in one of the hard currencies—including the United States dollar, Japanese yen, pound sterling, euro, Australian dollar, and Swiss franc—that typically give issuers relatively easier access to the capital markets. The top three issuance currencies—euro (42.6%), US dollar (33.4%), and Chinese yuan (7.7%)—represented 83.7% of overall sustainable debt issuance volume during the first quarters of 2021, similar to the 84%–90% share annually between 2016 and 2020. Most sustainability bonds in 2021 were issued in US dollars, while the share of other currencies remained small. This included a wide range of so-called soft currencies such as the Korean won and Malaysian ringgit. The social bond universe had greater diversity of currency issuance in 2020, with 70% of issuance in hard currencies and 30% in soft currencies. However, through the end of Q3 2021 hard currencies accounted for 96% of social debt issuance.

Regional Trends of Sustainable Finance in ASEAN+3

At the end of Q3 2021, the region's cumulative sustainable bonds outstanding reached USD463.7 billion. At least one GSS instrument had been issued in the majority of ASEAN+3 bond markets. According to the Climate Bonds database, the GSS debt market in 2020 and the first 3 quarters of 2021 was buoyed by social bonds issued as an immediate response to COVID-19 and by sustainability bond issuance in the first half of 2021 (Figure 2).[9] Overall, 556 GSS bonds and loans were issued in ASEAN+3 markets through the end of Q3 2021, down from the equivalent 9-month period in 2020 when 953 instruments were issued, of which 633 were labeled social-COVID-19 bonds. GSS bonds were already gaining traction before the onset of the pandemic and have continued to grow rapidly, with issuance in H1 2021 expanding 46.7% year-on-year (y-o-y) to USD82.3 billion, compared with H1 2020's total of USD56.0 billion (Table 3).

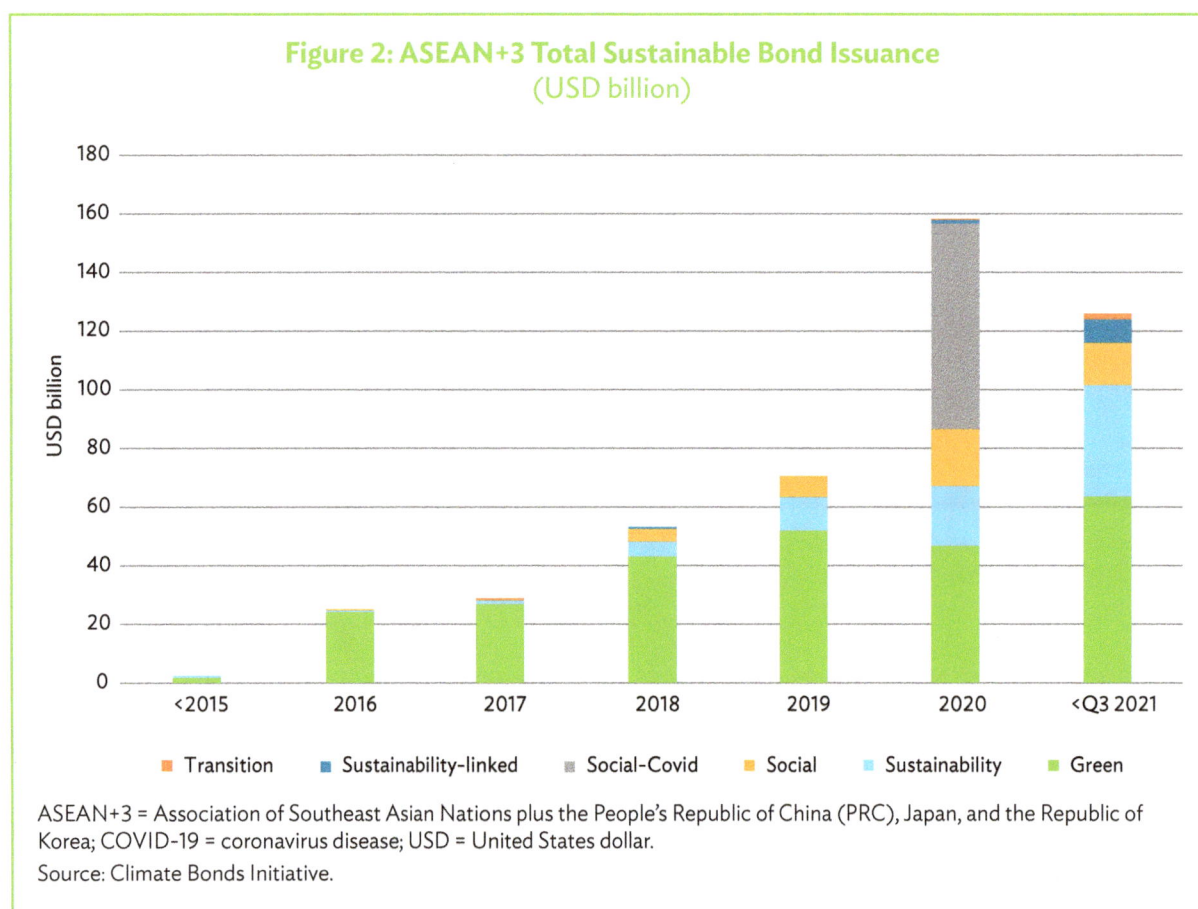

Figure 2: ASEAN+3 Total Sustainable Bond Issuance
(USD billion)

ASEAN+3 = Association of Southeast Asian Nations plus the People's Republic of China (PRC), Japan, and the Republic of Korea; COVID-19 = coronavirus disease; USD = United States dollar.
Source: Climate Bonds Initiative.

---

[9] Climate Bonds screens self-labeled debt instruments to identify bonds and similar debt instruments as eligible for inclusion in the respective Climate Bonds GSS bond databases. In some instances, self-labeled GSS instruments do not align with the Climate Bonds Taxonomy and are excluded from the respective Climate Bonds database. Hence, the market figures represented in this analysis may differ from those reported elsewhere.

Table 3: Annual Sustainable Bond Issuance
(USD billion)

Year	Green	Sustainability	Social	Social-COVID-19	Sustainability-Linked	Transition	Total
2015	1.8	0.7					2.5
2016	24.2	0.5	0.3				25.0
2017	26.9	1.2	0.2			0.5	28.7
2018	43.2	5.0	4.3	0.1	0.5		53.1
2019	51.9	11.3	7.1				70.3
2020	46.8	20.4	19.5	70.0	1.2	0.4	158.2
<Q3 2021	63.5	38.1	14.4		7.9	1.8	125.7
Total	**258.2**	**77.2**	**45.9**	**70.1**	**9.6**	**2.7**	**463.7**

USD = United States dollar.
Source: Climate Bonds Initiative.

Economy-Level Comparisons

In the ASEAN+3 region, the larger economies have driven the regional bond market's growth.[10] During the first 3 quarters of 2021, USD125.7 billion of GSS debt instruments were issued, with the PRC; the Republic of Korea; Hong Kong, China; and Japan responsible for 87.4% of that volume. Within ASEAN only, Singapore led with USD9.1 billion of issuance during the review period, followed by Thailand with USD3.4 billion, Indonesia with USD1.27 billion, and Malaysia with USD0.9 billion (Figure 3).

The regional GSS debt market was buoyant in 2020 and 2021, supported by social bonds issued in response to the pandemic in 2020 and by sustainability issuance in the first half of 2021. In Q1 2020, Chinese banks issued USD69 million in either social or "social-COVID-19" labeled bonds with an average tenor of 1.7 years. There were some notable differences in the types of GSS instruments being used between economies in the region. Those from Indonesia and Viet Nam have been predominantly green, while social bonds made up a large proportion of issuance from Malaysia and Hong Kong, China. Thailand saw significant green bond issuance together with other substantial sustainability, sustainability-linked and social bond volume. The Republic of Korea also embraced sustainability and social bond labels.

Figure 3: ASEAN+3 Sustainable Debt Issuance, January–September 2021
(USD billion)

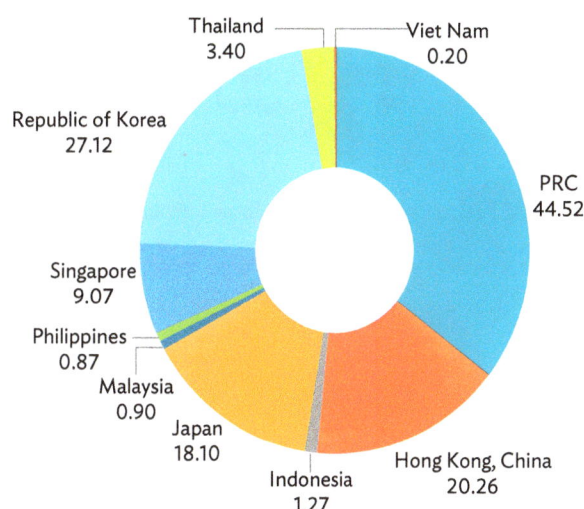

Thailand 3.40; Viet Nam 0.20; Republic of Korea 27.12; PRC 44.52; Singapore 9.07; Philippines 0.87; Malaysia 0.90; Japan 18.10; Indonesia 1.27; Hong Kong, China 20.26

ASEAN+3 = Association of Southeast Asian Nations, the People's Republic of China (PRC), Japan, and the Republic of Korea; USD = United States dollar.
Source: Climate Bonds Initiative.

[10] For the purposes of this report, the terms "country" and "economy" reflect the country or economy of the issuing entity. In Climate Bonds' global green bond database and statistics, "country" reflects the country or economy of risk, which may be different if the parent of the issuing entity is from another country or economy. For example, ICBC Singapore issued three green bonds in April 2019 totaling USD2.2 billion; these are classified as being issued in Singapore in this report but as from the PRC in the Climate Bonds database.

Recent Issuance Activity by Economy, Q1 2021–Q3 2021

The PRC remains the leader in ASEAN+3 sustainable bond issuance and was the source of USD44.5 billion in issuance during the first 9 months of 2021. More than half of this financing was earmarked for renewable energy and transport, which is especially pertinent in the aftermath of the PRC's 2060 carbon neutrality pledge (Figure 4).

Figure 4: Total Sustainable Bond Issuance in ASEAN+3 by Economy, Q1 2021–Q3 2021

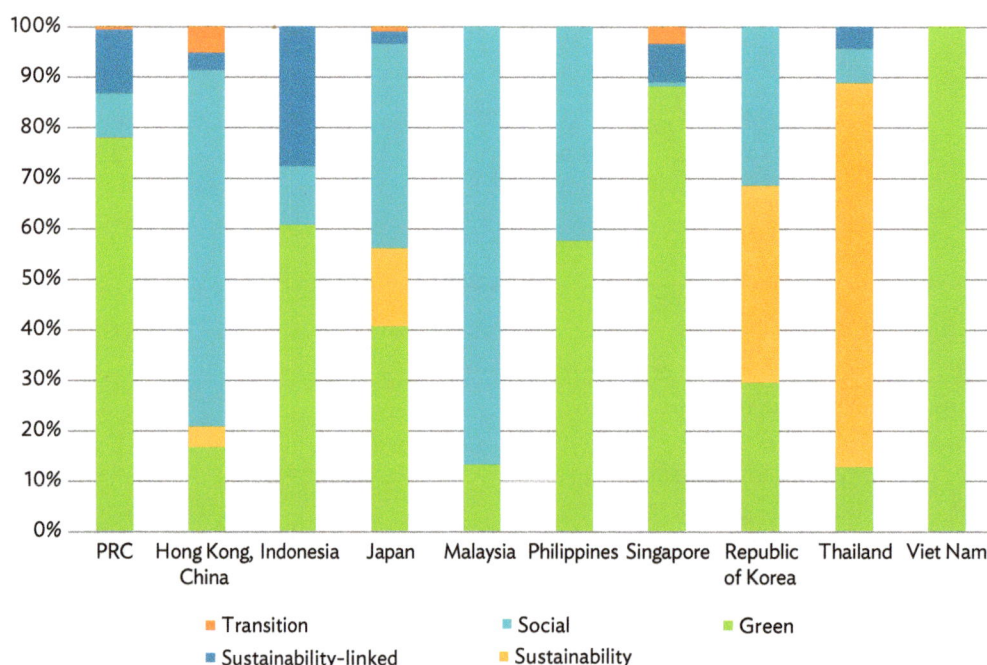

ASEAN+3 = Association of Southeast Asian Nations plus the People's Republic of China (PRC), Japan, and the Republic of Korea.
Source: Climate Bonds Initiative.

The PRC continues to innovate with GSS instruments. The Bank of China issued a blue bond in the international market in September 2020. Domestic demand quickly followed, and by June 2021, there were two blue bonds with a combined total value of CNY1.3 billion. In the first 9 months of 2021, carbon-neutral bond issuance in the PRC reached USD9.9 billion, accounting for 19.8% of the total amount of green bonds issued in the PRC during the review period. Bonds issued under the social theme included rural revitalization bonds (USD123.7 million) and pandemic bonds (USD68.0 billion), which together accounted for 28.2% of all Chinese GSS bond issuance in the review period.

The Republic of Korea had USD27.1 billion of total sustainable bond issuance in the first 3 quarters of 2021 and continued to be a key player in the region, having released its own Green Bond Guidelines in December 2020. Hong Kong, China had the third most sustainable bond issuance in the region during the review period with USD20.3 billion, followed by Japan with a total of USD18.1 billion. Singapore followed with USD9.1 billion in sustainable debt issued in the first 9 months of 2021. Thailand's issuance showed a preference for sustainability, green, and sustainability-linked bond bonds, which totaled USD3.5 billion. The Philippines issued USD872.0 million of sustainable bonds during the review period, while Malaysia showed a clear preference for social bond issuance among its total USD776 million of labeled debt raised. Viet Nam's breakdown of sustainable debt by type of bond is skewed by the fact that, during the first 3 quarters of 2021, it had only one green issue.

Issuance Volumes by Currency Type

LCY sustainable bonds debuted in the ASEAN+3 market in 2014, but issuance only really gathered pace in 2016; then, between 2017 and 2019, the market grew around 50% each year. In 2020, a spike in the share of LCY issuance can be attributed to the impact of large-scale, social-COVID-19 issuance in the PRC. LCY issuance in the first 3 quarters of 2021 was USD287.3 billion, representing 64% of the region's total sustainable debt issuance in ASEAN+3 (Figure 5).

Figure 5: ASEAN+3 Share of Local Currency in Sustainable Debt Issuances

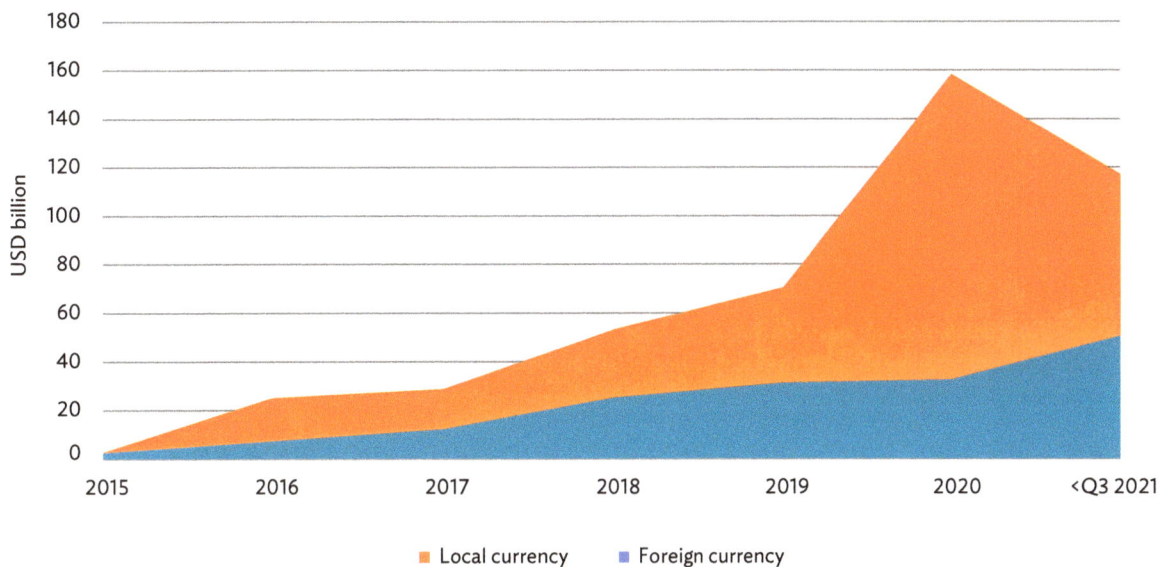

ASEAN+3 = Association of Southeast Asian Nations plus the People's Republic of China (PRC), Japan, and the Republic of Korea; USD = United States dollar.
Source: Climate Bonds Initiative.

LCY issuance comprised a majority share of all tenors of debt: 62.6% of long-term debt (>10 years), 58.5% of midterm debt (5–10 years), and 65.2% of short-term debt (<5 years). The fact that more than 60% of long-term debt is issued in local currencies can be attributed to domestic investor risk appetite given long-term fluctuations in foreign exchange markets, especially for long-term project finance. The preference for LCY short-term debt can also be drawn to its function as a vehicle for short-term liquidity relief, also lowering the risk for investors.

ASEAN+3 issuance demonstrates a preference for LCY debt for smaller instruments, making up 90% of issuances of less than USD200 million and 72.2% of issuances between USD200 million and USD500 million. The share of benchmark issuance (>USD500 million) appears reasonably balanced, with foreign currencies representing a slight majority (56.3%). This segment is dominated by Chinese and Japanese issuers, with a small but notable share made up of Singaporean real estate investment trusts.

Less than half of ASEAN+3 economies—the PRC, Japan, Malaysia, Singapore, and Thailand—account for a majority of the region's LCY sustainable debt issuance. Thailand stands out as having the largest share of LCY sustainable debt, with 98.5% of issuance (USD10.6 billion), bolstered by significant sovereign instruments denominated in Thai baht (Figure 6).

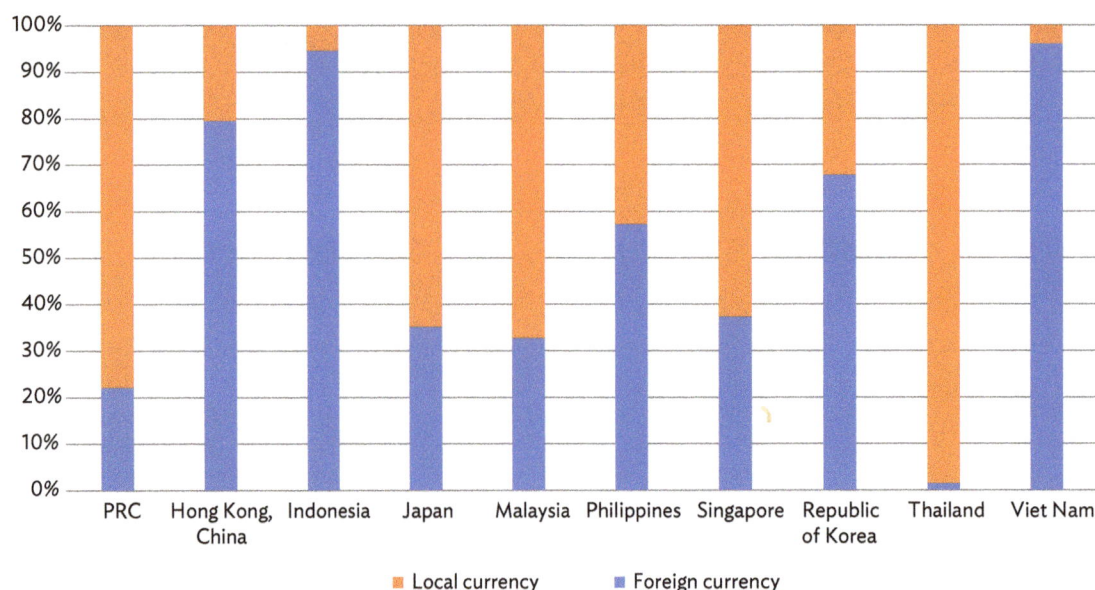

Figure 6: Share of Local Currency in ASEAN+3 Sustainable Debt Issuances by Economy

ASEAN+3 = Association of Southeast Asian Nations plus the People's Republic of China (PRC), Japan, and the Republic of Korea.
Note: Data reflects cumulative issuance through the end of September 2021.
Source: Climate Bonds Initiative.

Hong Kong, China; the Republic of Korea; Indonesia; the Philippines; and Viet Nam have issued a majority of their sustainable debt in foreign currencies. Viet Nam stands out as having almost the opposite share of sustainable debt as its neighbor Thailand, with 96.1% of debt (USD656.8 million) issued in foreign currencies. Indonesia has 94.6% of its debt denominated in foreign currencies, while the Philippines has a more balanced share of 53.9%.

People's Republic of China; Hong Kong, China; Japan; and the Republic of Korea

The PRC and Japan have each issued a majority of their sustainable debt in their respective domestic currency, totaling 77.8% and 64.9%, respectively. A minority issuance in euros and US dollars made up 3.8% and 16.3% of issuance in the PRC and Japan, respectively. The volume of CNY-denominated sustainable finance issuance in the PRC steadily rose from USD15.4 billion in 2017 to USD32.6 billion through the first 3 quarters of 2021, but the share fluctuated over that period, peaking in 2020 with the country's massive social-COVID-19 issuance.

Japan's largest foreign currency issuer is the Development Bank of Japan, which issued its first two green bonds worth EUR250 million and EUR300 million in 2014 and 2015, respectively. It has since exclusively issued under the sustainability label in both euros and US dollars, bringing the bank's overall issuance to a total of USD8.2 billion. The share of LCY sustainable debt in Japan has grown since its first issuance in 2014, reaching highs of 84.5% in 2019 and 79.2% in 2020.

The Republic of Korea and Hong Kong, China have most of their cumulative sustainable debt in foreign currencies, with total LCY issuance comprising shares of 32.2% and 20.5%, respectively. Hong Kong, China's share of LCY financing peaked in 2019 and fell to just 1.3% in Q3 2021. This was due in part to Hong Kong, China's green sovereign issuances in US dollars in both 2019 and 2021. The Republic of Korea has the opposite trend, with its share of LCY sustainable financing steadily rising since the first such issuance in 2016 (Figure 7).

Figure 7: Share of Local Currency Sustainable Debt Issuance in the People's Republic of China; Hong Kong, China; Japan; and the Republic of Korea

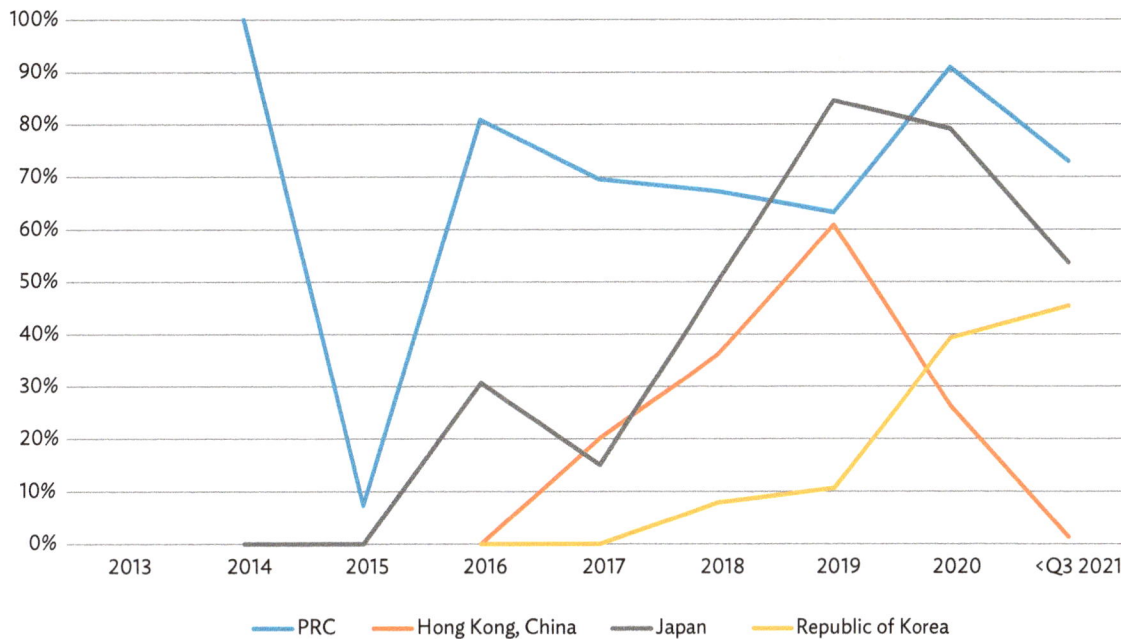

PRC = People's Republic of China.
Source: Climate Bonds Initiative.

Of the total sustainable debt issuance originating from these four economies, 24.6% was denominated in US dollars, with a USD-denominated low of about 16% of total issuance in the PRC and a high of about 67% in Hong Kong, China.

Association of Southeast Asian Nations

ASEAN issuance has grown rapidly since the region's first sustainable issuance in 2015 and was on track to reach new highs in 2021, having already surpassed the 2020 total of USD17.5 billion with USD18.3 billion through the end of Q3 2021. Green bond issuance dominates, representing USD10 billion of 2021 issuance through the end of September. Sustainability issuance followed with USD6.7 billion, while sustainability-linked bond issuance grew to USD1.2 billion in volume. The region's first transition-labeled issuance occurred in 2021 with a CNY2.0 billion (USD310 million) bond from China Construction Bank in April 2021 through its Singapore branch. The social bond segment remains in its infancy stage, however, with only USD546.2 million of total debt, and just USD90.0 million issued in the first 3 quarters of 2021 (Figure 8). Box 2 compares sustainable debt issuance in ASEAN with that of the Nordic countries to highlight the growth in such issuance in ASEAN since 2018.

ASEAN saw a few important issuances in 2021, notably Indonesia's fifth sovereign *sukuk* (Islamic bond) worth USD750 million under its green *sukuk* program, which it launched in 2018. Malaysia issued the world's first USD-denominated sovereign sustainability *sukuk* in April 2021, which was worth USD1.3 billion and aligned with the UN SDGs. Singapore's National Environment Agency issued its first green bond in September 2021 worth SGD1.65 billion (USD1.23 billion).

Figure 8: Sustainable Debt Issuance by ASEAN Members

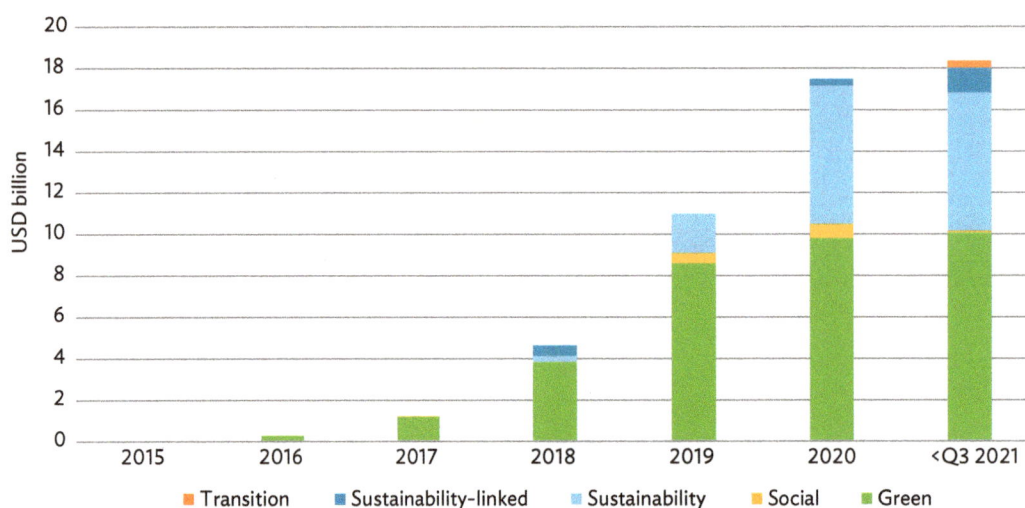

ASEAN = Association of Southeast Asian Nations, USD = United States dollar.
Source: Climate Bonds Initiative.

Of the six ASEAN economies that have issued sustainable debt thus far, a majority of such issuances in Singapore, Malaysia, and Thailand were LCY-denominated with shares of 62.3%, 67.3%, and 98.5%, respectively.

Conversely, Indonesia, the Philippines, and Viet Nam have issued the majority of their respective sustainable debt in foreign currencies (Figure 9). The Philippines has a small majority in foreign currency (53.9%), while Indonesia and Viet Nam have strong majorities in foreign currency, with just 5.4% and 4.0% issued in local currency, respectively.

Figure 9: Sustainable Debt Issuance by ASEAN Members

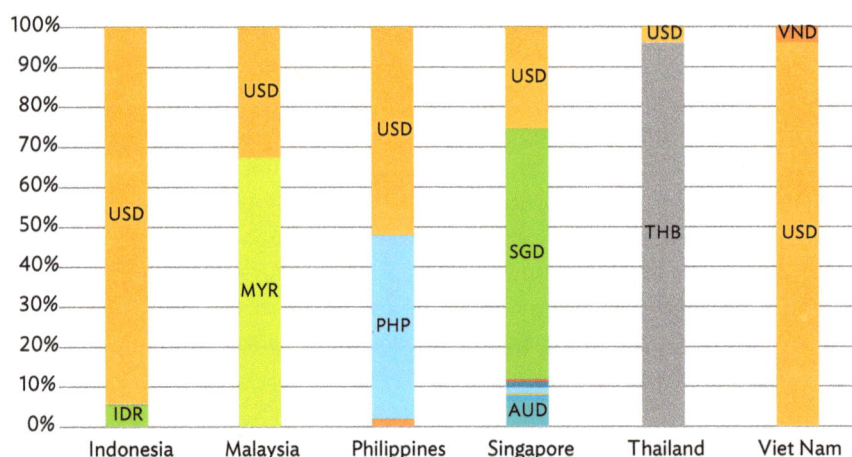

ASEAN = Association of Southeast Asian Nations, AUD = Australian dollar, CHF = Swiss franc, CNY = Chinese yuan, EUR = euro, GBP = pound sterling, IDR = Indonesian rupiah, INR = Indian rupee, JPY = Japanese yen, MYR = Malaysian ringgit, PHP = Philippine peso, SGD = Singapore dollar, THB = Thai baht, USD = United States dollar, VND = Vietnamese dong.
Source: Climate Bonds Initiative.

Box 2: Comparing Sustainable Debt Issuance in ASEAN and Nordic Countries

The overall volume of sustainable debt in the Association of Southeast Asian Nations (ASEAN) has been growing rapidly. In comparison to the five Nordic countries—Denmark, Finland, Iceland, Norway, and Sweden—ASEAN local currency (LCY) sustainable debt has grown from just 7% of the Nordic countries' sustainable LCY debt pre-2018 to 54% in the first 3 quarters of 2021.

Figure: Local Currency Sustainable Debt Volume— ASEAN versus Nordic Countries

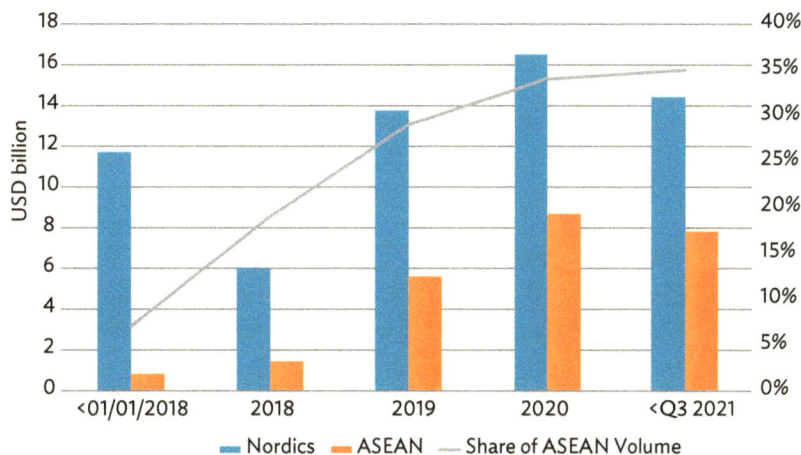

ASEAN = Association of Southeast Asian Nations, USD = United States dollar.
Note: The Nordic grouping comprises Denmark, Finland, Iceland, Norway, and Sweden.
Source: Climate Bonds Initiative.

Table: Comparison of Local Currency Sustainable Debt Markets: Nordic Countries versus ASEAN

Period	ASEAN Market Size (USD million)	ASEAN+3 Market Size (USD billion)	Nordic Countries Market Size (USD million)	Relative Size: ASEAN to Nordic
<2018	810 m	34.8	11,700 m	7%
2018	1,420 m	28.0	6,000 m	24%
2019	5,580 m	39.2 bn	13,750 m	41%
2020	8,680 m	125.7 bn	16,490 m	53%
<Q3 2021	7,810 m	66.0 bn	14,430 m	54%

ASEAN = Association of Southeast Asian Nations, USD = United States dollar.
Source: Climate Bonds Initiative.

While Thailand's LCY vanilla bond market is larger than Sweden's, and Indonesia's is larger than Norway's, this is not the case for the sustainable LCY bond market.[a] Despite the rapid growth of sustainable debt volumes in ASEAN, Thailand's USD10.8 billion of sustainable debt issuance during the review period was just 18.0% of Sweden's USD60.3 billion, and Indonesia's USD7.6 billion of sustainable debt issuance was just 28.6% of Norway's USD26.7 billion. While ASEAN's growth has been steady and consistent, there is still policy space to improve the scale of its sustainable debt markets.

[a] Bloomberg. 2020. Vanilla Bond Market Sizes 2020.
Source: Climate Bonds Initiative.

Green Bond Pricing in the Primary Market

Climate Bonds has been tracking green bond pricing in the primary market since 2017. This work has been limited to instruments denominated in US dollar or euro with a minimum initial issue size of USD500 million. A bond may be issued at a higher price, resulting in a lower yield. This type of bond would sit inside the issuer's yield curve (which is known as a new issue concession); when used in conjunction with a green bond, Climate Bonds refers to this as a "greenium." This is a favorable outcome for any issuer because it means that its green bond will cost less to fund than its vanilla debt.

Green bonds are subject to the same market dynamics as vanilla bonds, including supply, rate expectations, geopolitical concerns, and the aftermath of global pandemics. Despite the additional monetary costs and time investment, the exercise of issuing green bonds is widely perceived as valuable.

This research has not extended to peripheral currencies. Data availability and transparency and scale requirements mean there is not sufficient critical mass for comparison. Of the few LCY benchmark-sized deals available in ASEAN+3, analysis is prohibited by a lack of data or transparency on similar vanilla bonds, both of which are crucial components of this analysis. However, the Republic of Korea is a notable source of benchmark USD-denominated green bonds from multiple issuers. Nonetheless, one notable example was the issuance of Thailand's inaugural Sustainability Bond in 2020, which matched strong demand from investors with an amount submitted totaling THB60,911 million, which was 3.05 times the announced offering, and attracted an interest rate of 1.585%, which was lower than the market yield of the existing 15-year benchmark bond.

Green Bond Pricing in H1 2021

According to Climate Bonds' paper *Green Bond Pricing in the Primary Market H1 2021*, investors were naturally concerned about inflation and wary of overpaying for assets that could be impacted by rising interest rates. In H1 2021, however, rates remained low, and technical factors such as continued central bank support and the effects of other pandemic support contributed to rising bond prices. In H1 2021, corporate bond spreads narrowed and the spreads of broad market BBB indices tightened by 17 percentage points in both euros and dollars. Green bond issuance soared globally and in ASEAN+3 during this time, setting new monthly highs in the first half of 2021.[11]

In H1 2021, qualifying green bonds denominated in euro and US dollar attracted larger book cover and exhibited larger spread compression on average compared to their vanilla equivalents. For EUR-denominated bonds, the average oversubscription was 2.9x for green and 2.6x for vanilla, while USD-denominated bonds had a much larger difference (4.7x green and 2.5x vanilla). This applies to spread compression too: for EUR-denominated bonds it was 20.4 basis points (bps) for green and 19.6 bps for vanilla; for USD-denominated bonds, it was 29.9 bps for green and 24.8 bps for vanilla (Figure 10).

In H1 2021, eight USD-denominated green bonds from ASEAN+3 issuers qualified (Figure 11). On average, those bonds had a book cover of 5.7x, compared to 2.5x for vanilla equivalents. Sumitomo Mitsui Trust Bank, for example, priced its second green bond in March 2021, a 5-year USD500 million bond that covered its book by 7.2 times. The bond was part of a two-tranche deal, with the larger portion having a USD1.75 billion 3-year maturity and a 1.7x book cover. It has been suggested that, regardless of UOP, smaller deals will always attract a book cover with higher multiples. While this may be true in this case, the green deal received a USD3.6 billion commitment, compared to USD3.0 billion for the vanilla deal.

---

11   Climate Bonds Initiative. 2021. *Green Bond Pricing in the Primary Market H1 2021*. London.

Figure 10: United States Dollar Green Bonds in ASEAN+3 Achieved Higher Book Cover than Vanilla Equivalents

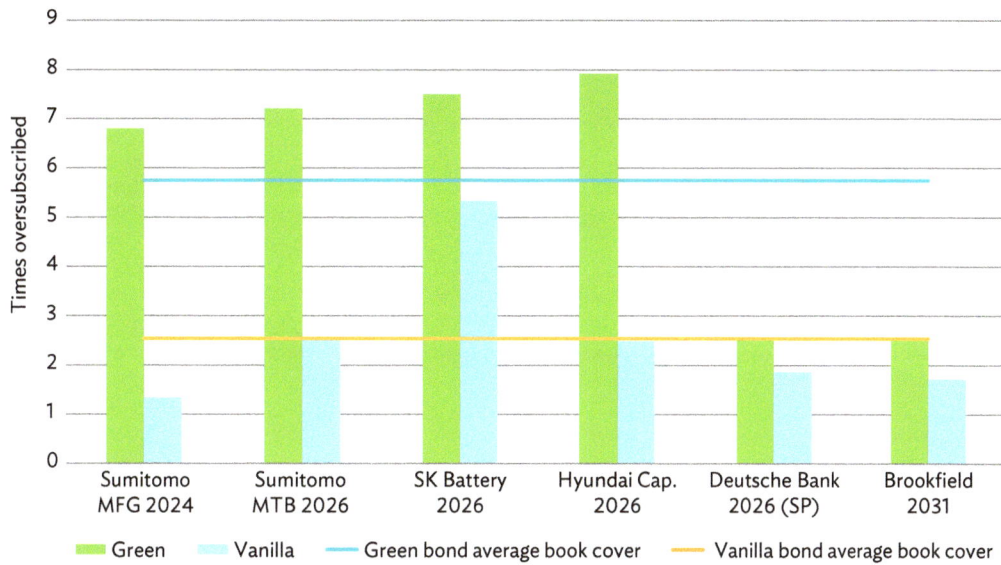

ASEAN+3 = Association of Southeast Asian Nations plus the People's Republic of China, Japan, and the Republic of Korea.
Source: Climate Bonds Initiative.

Figure 11: United States Dollar-Denominated Green Bonds Achieved Greater Spread Compression than Vanilla Bonds in the ASEAN+3 Basket

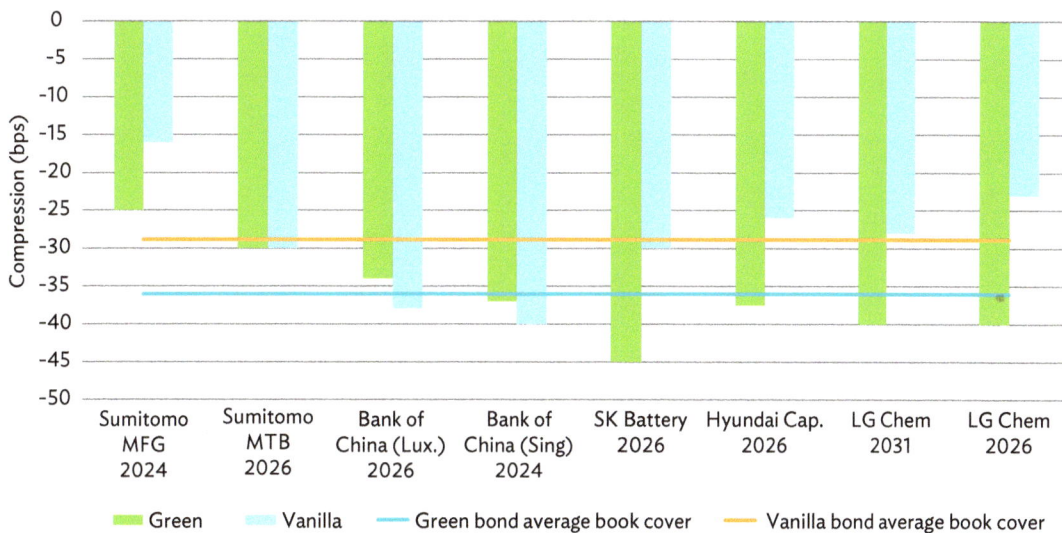

ASEAN+3 = Association of Southeast Asian Nations plus the People's Republic of China, Japan, and the Republic of Korea; bps = basis points.
Note: Sample of ASEAN+3 countries from the original global basket.
Source: Climate Bonds Initiative.

On the spread compression, SK Battery 2026 experienced the most aggressive tightening of 45 bps during book building. At the end of June, LG Chem issued two green bonds, each worth USD500 million and due in 2026 and 2031, respectively. During the book-building process, both bonds tightened by 40 bps.

Sovereign Spotlight

Sovereign issuers can bolster the green bond market's scale, liquidity, momentum, and profile, while also providing a critical source of capital for achieving the goals of the Paris Agreement. With the addition of two new EUR-denominated and four new USD-denominated sovereign green bonds to the Climate Bonds Green Bond Database in H1 2021, the sovereign green bond club continues to grow.

These included the fourth green *sukuk* from Indonesia, a 2051 USD750 million bond in June 2021 (Figure 12). Indonesia—having previously issued green *sukuk* in 2018 (USD1.25 billion 2023), 2019 (USD750 million 2024), and 2020 (USD750 million 2025)—is the largest issuer of green labeled *sukuk*.

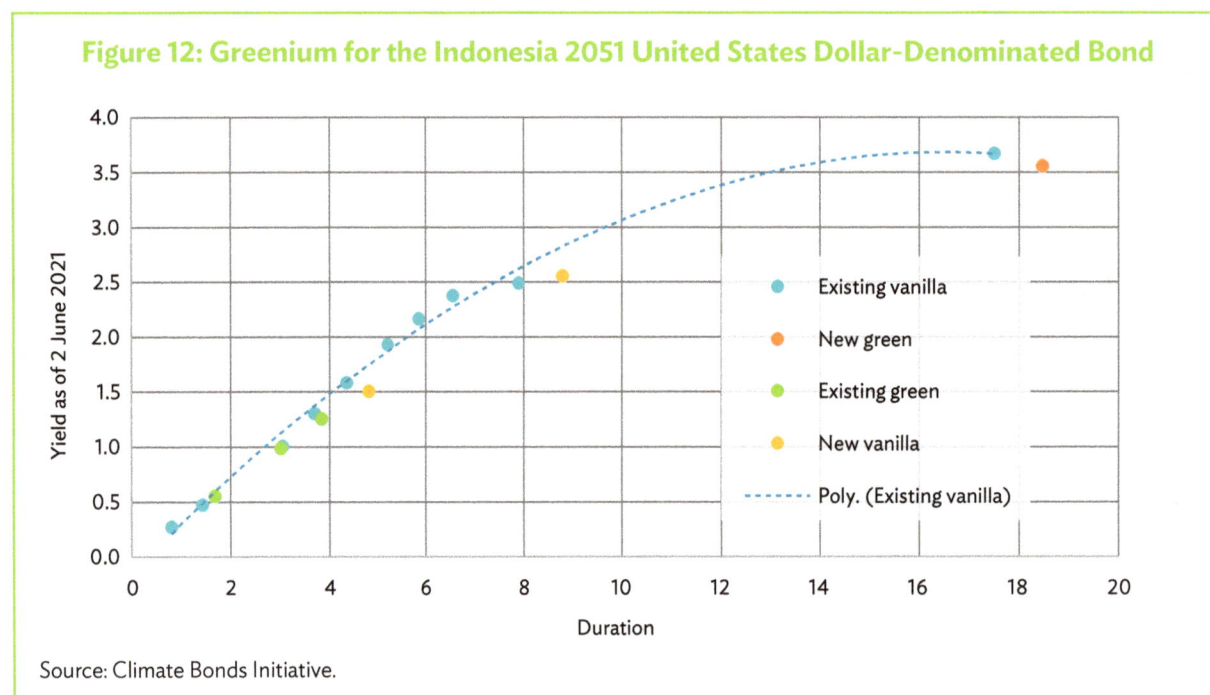

Figure 12: Greenium for the Indonesia 2051 United States Dollar-Denominated Bond

Source: Climate Bonds Initiative.

The fourth green *sukuk*, like previous Indonesian green *sukuk*, had strong primary market dynamics. It received a 4.5x book cover and was priced in greenium. The green yield curve remained inside the vanilla curve a month later (Figure 13). Green investors made up 57% of the total, a significant increase from the 34% achieved for Indonesia's last green bond, which was issued in 2020.

Figure 13: Indonesia's Green Curve Inside Vanilla Curve (+1 month)

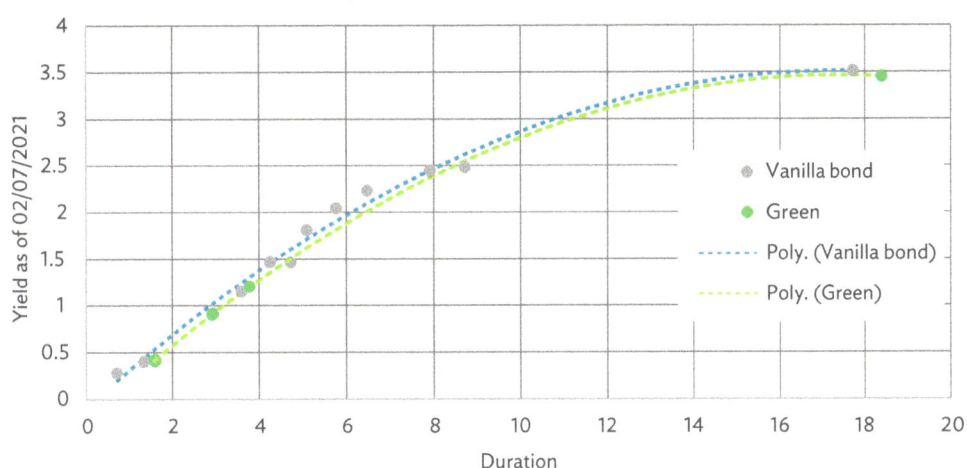

Source: Climate Bonds Initiative.

Current Initiatives on Transition Finance in ASEAN+3

The transition debt finance market in ASEAN+3 gained traction in 2020–2021. Transition-labeled UOP bonds in the region represent about USD1.7 billion of value and originate from five issuers: China Construction Bank, Bank of China, Castle Peak Power Finance, NYK Line, and Seaspan Corp. The issuers are from the PRC; Hong Kong, China; Japan; and Singapore.[12]

The SLB market in ASEAN+3, while also novel, has shown faster growth in its issuance volumes. SLBs represent about USD9.6 billion of debt. This market is dominated by the PRC but includes notable issuance volumes from Hong Kong, China; Japan; Indonesia; Thailand; and Singapore.

Transition bonds allow responsible investors to support businesses or activities transitioning to low- or zero-carbon operations, particularly in traditionally high-carbon industries. Transition bonds are more inclusive because the proceeds can be used to fund transition activities or general corporate purposes, as long as the entire company is in the process of transitioning.

The groundwork has been laid for transition finance in the region. In May 2021, Japan's Financial Services Agency released its guidelines for the sector, based on ICMA's *Climate Transition Finance Handbook*.[13] Also, Singapore's Green Finance Industry Taskforce released a white paper in May 2021, outlining ways to mitigate barriers to financing transition activities.[14] Further developments are taking place elsewhere in the region. For instance, Malaysia's recent Climate Change and Principle-Based Taxonomy (CCPT) includes transition finance, identifying it as one of three sustainability categories.[15]

---

[12]   In line with countries included in the Climate Bonds Green Bond Database Methodology.
[13]   Government of Japan, Financial Services Agency. 2021. "Basic Guidelines on Climate Transition Finance" Announced. News release. 24 May. https://www.fsa.go.jp/en/news/2021/20210524.html.
[14]   Green Finance Industry Taskforce. 2021. White Paper on Fostering Green Finance Solutions. 19 May. https://abs.org.sg/docs/library/fostering-green-finance-solutions-white-paper.pdf.
[15]   Bank Negara Malaysia. 2021. Climate Change and Principle-based Taxonomy. News release. 30 April. https://www.bnm.gov.my/-/climate-change-principle-based-taxonomy.

The ASEAN Taxonomy Board established by four sectorial bodies under the ASEAN finance cooperation process—the ASEAN Capital Markets Forum (ACMF), ASEAN Insurance Regulators' Meeting, ASEAN Senior Level Committee on Financial Integration, and ASEAN Working Committee on Capital Market Development—published the *ASEAN Taxonomy for Sustainable Finance (Version 1)* in November 2021 to drive the region's sustainability agenda and to facilitate an orderly transition toward a sustainable ASEAN. (See the section in this paper on Policies and Approaches to Promote Local Currency Sustainable Finance in ASEAN+3 for further details.)

Pathway toward Transition Finance

To ensure that the region can reduce GHG emissions, better hedge against climate change risks, and thrive in the long run, it must transition to a green, climate-resilient economy. Though GSS bond markets continue to grow, the transition is not yet taking place at a large enough scale or at a fast enough pace to meet the Paris Agreement's objectives.

The need to standardize definitions and ambition levels for what is classified and labeled as transition finance still exists. The Climate Bonds discussion paper, *Transition Finance for Transforming Companies,* highlights five hallmarks of a credibly transitioning company as shown in Figure 14.[16]

These five hallmarks lay the foundation for the assessment and certification of instruments like SLBs—with their forward-looking, company-wide targets—for transition-labeled UOP bonds, as well as for broader assessments of the integrity of a company's transition.

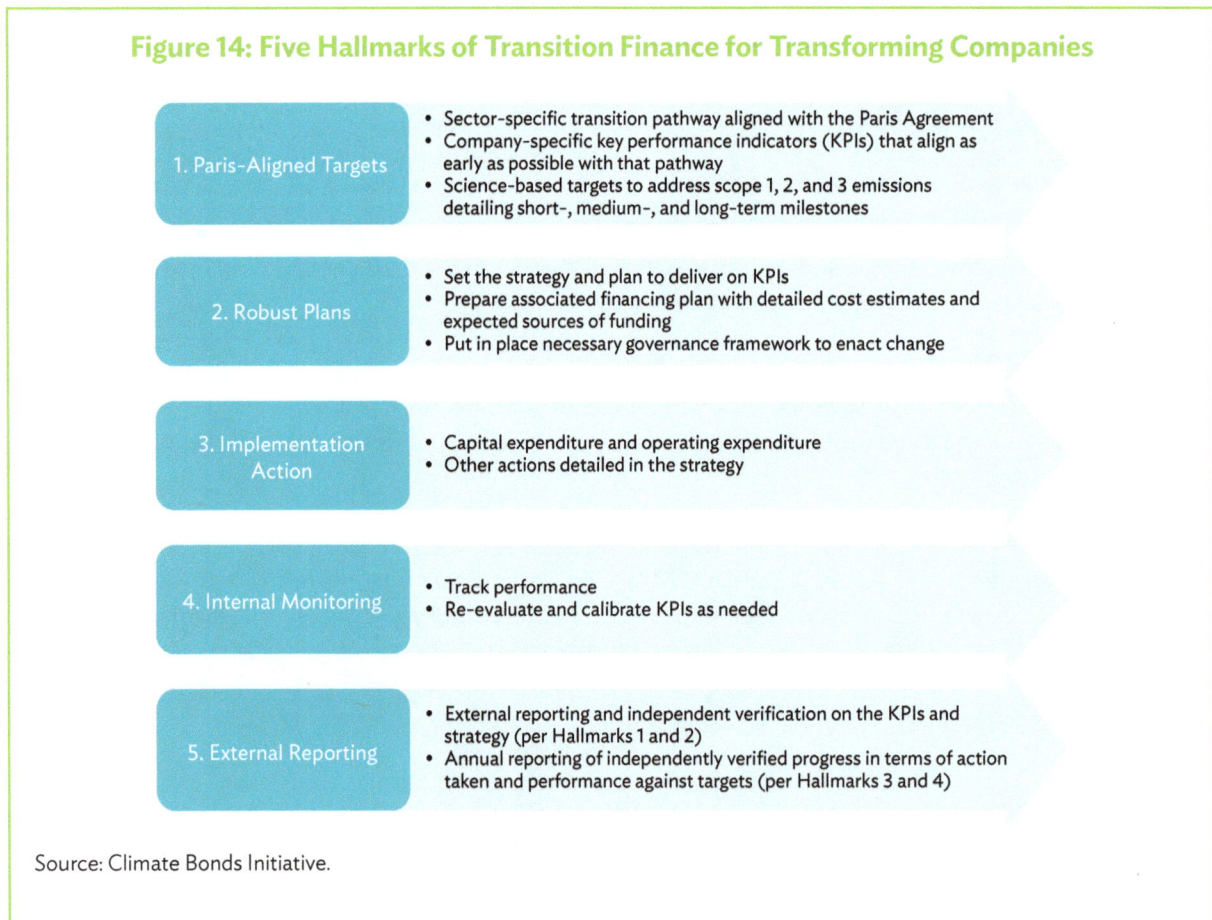

Figure 14: Five Hallmarks of Transition Finance for Transforming Companies

1. Paris-Aligned Targets
- Sector-specific transition pathway aligned with the Paris Agreement
- Company-specific key performance indicators (KPIs) that align as early as possible with that pathway
- Science-based targets to address scope 1, 2, and 3 emissions detailing short-, medium-, and long-term milestones

2. Robust Plans
- Set the strategy and plan to deliver on KPIs
- Prepare associated financing plan with detailed cost estimates and expected sources of funding
- Put in place necessary governance framework to enact change

3. Implementation Action
- Capital expenditure and operating expenditure
- Other actions detailed in the strategy

4. Internal Monitoring
- Track performance
- Re-evaluate and calibrate KPIs as needed

5. External Reporting
- External reporting and independent verification on the KPIs and strategy (per Hallmarks 1 and 2)
- Annual reporting of independently verified progress in terms of action taken and performance against targets (per Hallmarks 3 and 4)

Source: Climate Bonds Initiative.

---

16   Climate Bonds Initiative. 2021. *Transition Finance for Transforming Companies.* London.

3

Policies and Approaches to Promote Local Currency Sustainable Finance

Summary of the Regional Experience

LCY capital markets in the ASEAN+3 region are at various stages of development across member economies; respective legal and policy frameworks vary, as does the extent of sustainable finance market development. Notwithstanding, ASEAN+3 policymakers have joined hands to facilitate the development of LCY sustainable bond markets and the promotion of financial cooperation toward integration across the region.[17]

However, a lack of understanding as to what types of assets and projects qualify for green financing is evident. Market actors must be provided with an explicit and science-based definition of green that can support better-informed and more efficient decision-making. ASEAN+3 economies have dedicated their efforts to the development of a green taxonomy that guides the overall financial market. The first green taxonomy introduced in the region is the *Green Bond Endorsed Project Catalogue* introduced by the PRC in 2015, followed by Malaysia's *Climate Change and Principle-Based Taxonomy* in April 2021.[18,19] Japan released its *Basic Guidelines on Climate Transition Finance* in May 2021, which may serve as a basis for a future transition taxonomy.[20] Outside these developments, other taxonomies (e.g., those of the Republic of Korea, Viet Nam, Singapore, and Thailand) are still in the development phase.[21]

ASEAN+3 policymakers are making a continued effort to build a concrete green bond policy framework while trying to lay the groundwork for other thematic bonds in recognition of the negative effects of the COVID-19 pandemic and the demand for projects with environmental and social co-benefits. To complement the *ASEAN Green Bond Standards,* initially released in November 2017, the ACMF also introduced the *ASEAN Social Bond Standards* and *ASEAN Sustainability Bond Standards* in 2018, contributing to the development of a new asset class with social and environmental and social co-benefits, reducing due diligence costs, and helping investors to make informed investment decisions.[22] These standards will be a common language for all ASEAN member economies and ensure the ASEAN region will move together as a whole.

In partnership with ADB, the ACMF also developed the *Roadmap for ASEAN Sustainable Capital Markets,* which aims to develop an open and vibrant ASEAN capital markets ecosystem that facilitates and mobilizes the private sector in the financing of sustainable projects.[23] Key priorities in the region pointed out in the roadmap include strengthening the foundations around sustainability reporting and transparency, identifying ways to systematically

---

[17] ADB. 2018. *Promoting Green Local Currency Bonds for Infrastructure Development in ASEAN+3.* Manila. https://www.adb.org/sites/default/files/publication/410326/green-lcy-bonds-infrastructure-development-asean3.pdf.

[18] The taxonomy is called the Green Bond Endorsed Project catalogue or the Green Bond Catalogue. It is updated regularly and the most updated version to date is from 2021.

[19] Climate Bonds Initiative. Notice on Issuing the Green Bond Endorsed Projects Catalogue (2021 Edition). https://www.climatebonds.net/files/files/the-Green-Bond-Endorsed-Project-Catalogue-2021-Edition-110521.pdf.

[20] UN Environment Programme. Policy Info: Taxonomy in Asia. https://www.unepfi.org/regions/asia-pacific/taxonomy-asia/.

[21] Government of Japan, Financial Services Agency; Ministry of Economy, Trade and Industry; and Ministry of the Environment. 2021. *Basic Guidelines on Climate Transition Finance.* https://www.meti.go.jp/press/2021/05/20210507001/20210507001-3.pdf.

[22] ACMF. 2018. *ASEAN Sustainability Bond Standards.* https://www.sc.com.my/api/documentms/download.ashx?id=3c4f768f-a290-4722-b9d1-ef55942fbfde.

[23] ACMF. *Roadmap for ASEAN Sustainable Capital Markets.* https://www.theacmf.org/images/downloads/pdf/ACMF_Roadmap_high.resolution.pdf.

embed sustainable finance practices in capital markets, capacity building, and strengthening partnerships and networks.[24]

The recently released *ASEAN Taxonomy for Sustainable Finance (Version 1)* is designed to be inclusive of the different starting points of ASEAN economies, and it encapsulates all the key components of a sustainable finance taxonomy that is tailored to address the needs of all members while being credible at the same time. Version 1 focused on setting out the conceptual framework for the plus standard via an intentional phased approach. Given the varying stages of development across the region, technical thresholds or quantitative screening criteria were not included in the first iteration of the taxonomy. Hence, Version 1 provides the key concepts of the taxonomy as a basis for consultation, discussion, and collaboration as the ASEAN Taxonomy Board develops the taxonomy further. Follow-up work is likely to be convened in 2022 to put forward thresholds to be developed into a full taxonomy. Currently, there are two parts of the taxonomy:

- **Foundation framework.** The classification of activities is qualitative. A decision tree classifies activities as either green, amber (transition), or red (excluded);
- **Plus standard framework.** This will contain quantitative screening criteria at the activity level.

The plus standard framework will have multiple thresholds set for each activity, with a scenario of three thresholds illustrated in Version 1. The need for flexibility was necessary to ensure inclusivity across all participating economies in a complex region with a complex taxonomy. International investors are yet to express clear views on this development; however, the Version 1 document recognizes that the complexity created by including multiple tiers may require additional efforts for users to understand. Nevertheless, the advantage of this system is that it takes into consideration the different starting points of emissions generated by different entities for the same activity.

ASEAN central banks also collaborated on a report describing their roles in managing climate and environment-related risks to better understand the implications of climate risk on the ASEAN financial sector and economy.[25] It provides a set of nonbinding recommendations to the central banks on safeguarding financial stability while supporting a low-carbon transition. Several ASEAN central banks are already acting. The ASEAN central banks also endorsed the initiative on ASEAN Sustainable Banking Principles in March 2021. These will serve as guiding principles for the development of sustainable banking guidelines.[26]

The ASEAN Infrastructure Fund (AIF) is a dedicated fund established in 2011 by ASEAN members and ADB to address the ASEAN region's infrastructure development needs by mobilizing regional savings, including foreign exchange reserves. All AIF-financed infrastructure projects are also cofinanced by ADB. The AIF is an integral part of ASEAN's efforts to strengthen regional connectivity.[27] The AIF has committed an estimated USD517 million for 11 projects, with a total portfolio size of around USD3.0 billion, including ADB cofinancing.

In April 2019, the AIF launched the ASEAN Catalytic Green Finance Facility (ACGF), which leverages resources from the AIF, ADB, and other development partners to accelerate the development of green infrastructure in Southeast Asia and bridge bankability gaps.[28] By June 2021, the ACGF was mainstreamed as a permanent facility under the AIF ahead of the end of its pilot phase. This was the result of a successful pilot period that demonstrated the ACGF's ability to originate and support development of green projects and leverage financing for them. The ACGF met or exceeded five of the six targets set in the 2019–2021 operational plan. The ACGF's early achievements

[24] ACMF. Roadmap for ASEAN Sustainable Capital Markets. https://www.theacmf.org/initiatives/sustainable-finance/roadmap-for-asean-sustainable-capital-markets.

[25] ASEAN. Report on The Roles of ASEAN Central Banks in Managing Climate and Environment-related Risks. https://asean.org/book/report-on-the-roles-of-asean-central-banks-in-managing-climate-and-environment-related-risks.

[26] International Finance Corporation. 2021. Sustainable Banking Network (Overview). https://www.ifc.org/wps/wcm/connect/98ed795e-559a-496c-b76d-b89ddb8c2716/SBN_Brief+20210511.pdf?MOD=AJPERES&CVID=nBpj8ZX.

[27] ADB. ASEAN Infrastructure Fund. https://www.adb.org/what-we-do/funds/asean-infrastructure-fund.

[28] ADB. 2019. ASEAN Catalytic Green Finance Facility. Manila. https://www.adb.org/sites/default/files/publication/544486/asean-catalytic-green-finance-facility.pdf.

have cemented its role as a key player supporting a green, resilient, and inclusive recovery in Southeast Asia after the coronavirus disease (COVID-19) pandemic. In 2021, ADB took an important step forward for Southeast Asia in the pursuit of green and inclusive recovery from the COVID-19 pandemic by launching an ACGF-managed Green Recovery Platform to support ASEAN member countries' efforts to realize their climate ambitions in the face of increased climate and economic vulnerability (Box 3).[29]

Box 3: Green Recovery Platform in Southeast Asia

During 2021, the Asian Development Bank (ADB) launched the Association of Southeast Asian Nations (ASEAN) Green Recovery Platform, which will support the objectives of the ASEAN Catalytic Green Finance Facility (ACGF). Four partners have pledged a total of USD665 million to this effort, including the Green Climate Fund (USD300 million), Italy's state lender Cassa Depositi e Prestiti (equivalent of USD155 million), the Government of the United Kingdom (USD151 million), and the European Union (USD59 million).

The platform will help develop and finance post-coronavirus disease (COVID-19) green infrastructure with significant benefits in creating green jobs to support economic recovery. It collates funding support from climate donors and cofinanciers, to support Southeast Asia developing member countries to focus on the implementation of their green finance pathways within the context of a COVID-19 recovery. For this purpose, it will provide concessional loans and technical assistance to help develop and finance a pipeline of green projects in ASEAN.

These new partnerships complement about USD1.4 billion in cofinancing already pledged to the ACGF by ADB, Agence Française de Développement, European Investment Bank, German state-owned development bank KfW, and the Government of the Republic of Korea, bringing indicative support to over USD2 billion.

Source: ACGF.

A summary of recent key policies and developments in ASEAN are detailed in Table 8.

Table 4: Recent Key Policies and Developments in ASEAN

Policy	Date	Lead Organization	Description	Link
ASEAN Green Bond Standards	2017	ACMF	Facilitate ASEAN capital markets in tapping green finance to support sustainable regional growth	Source
ASEAN Social Bond Standards	2018	ACMF	Enhance transparency, consistency, and uniformity of ASEAN social bonds	Source
ASEAN Sustainability Bond Standards	2018	ACMF	Guide the issuance of ASEAN sustainability bonds	Source
ASEAN Catalytic Green Finance Facility	2019	ASEAN Infrastructure Fund	Accelerate green infrastructure projects and bridge bankability gaps	Source
ASEAN Taskforce's Report on the Roles of ASEAN Central Banks in Managing Climate and Environment-Related Risks	2020	ASEAN central banks and monetary authorities collaboration	Set of nonbinding recommendations for increased disclosure and calling for the implementation of an ASEAN Green Map for financial services	Source
Roadmap for ASEAN Sustainable Capital Markets	2020	ACMF	Strategic direction and recommendations to guide ACMF and its members in developing action plans and initiatives	Source

continued on next page

---

[29] ADB. 2022. *ASEAN Catalytic Green Finance Facility 2021: Financing for a Green Recovery in Southeast Asia.* Manila. https://www.adb.org/documents/asean-catalytic-green-finance-facility-2021.

Table 4 *continued*

Policy	Date	Lead Organization	Description	Link
Report on Promoting Sustainable Finance in ASEAN	2020	Working Committee on Capital Market Development	Develop recommendations on policies for sustainable finance development in ASEAN, emphasizing the importance of coordination, market awareness, and education	Source
ASEAN Taxonomy for Sustainable Finance (Version 1)	2021	ASEAN Taxonomy Board	Develop, maintain, and promote a multitiered ASEAN Taxonomy for Sustainable Finance	Source
ASEAN Central Banks' initiative on ASEAN Sustainable Banking Principles	Undetermined	ASEAN central banks collaboration	Guiding principles to help ASEAN central banks further develop sustainable banking guidelines	Source
ASEAN Green Recovery Platform (under the ACGF)	2021	ADB	Kickstart green investments and help design governments' green stimulus packages	Source

ACGF = ASEAN Catalytic Green Finance Facility, ACMF = ASEAN Capital Markets Forum, ADB = Asian Development Bank, ASEAN = Association of Southeast Asian Nations.
Source: Author's compilation.

People's Republic of China

Following the announcement of the PRC's commitment to achieve carbon neutrality by 2060, top policymakers and regulators increased incentives for market participants to factor environmental, social, and climate considerations into their investment decisions. Nonetheless, the inconsistencies between the UOP rules and the regulations governing green external review providers are still being explored. The PRC's Five-Year Plan for Carbon Emissions Reduction, the updated *Green Bond Endorsed Projects Catalogue (2021 Edition)*, and the *Green Financial Performance Evaluation Plan for Banking Depository Financial Institutions* are all significant policy developments.[30] The People's Bank of China (PBOC) has also announced further work in other areas: mandatory disclosure, climate stress tests, "greening" of foreign exchange reserves, and encouraging financial institutions to invest in environmental, social, and governance (ESG) products and the domestic carbon market.[31]

The process of developing the PRC's green taxonomies has been strongly influenced by the existing structure of the country's financial market, which is dominated by the banking sector and supervised by multiple governmental bodies with multiple systems of regulation and various regulatory concepts, operation mechanisms, and regulatory styles.[32]

Different types of debt financing instruments are regulated by different regulators, which also tend to set varying rules regarding definitions of green, UOP, verification, and reporting. This means that, for example, a bond issued by a financial institution is overseen by the China Banking and Insurance Regulatory Commission (CBIRC) and the PBOC, while a bond issued by a large state-owned enterprise is subject to approval by the National Development

---

[30]   Climate Bonds Initiative. 2021. *China Green Securitization State of the Market 2020 report*. https://www.climatebonds.net/resources/reports/china-green-securitization-state-market-2020-report.

[31]   Banque de France. 2021. Green Finance in the Asia-Pacific Region: Mobilisation Spearheaded by Central Banks and Supervisory Authorities. *Banque de France Bulletin*. Paris.

[32]   For example, the issuance of financial bonds (Jinrongzhai 金融债) is approved by the People's Bank of China (PBOC), whereas the corporate bonds (Qiyezhai 企业债) should first be applied by the issuer company, approved by the NDRC, and countersigned by the PBOC and CSRC with the final issue permits been granted. The company bond (Gongsizhai 公司债), on the other hand, is required to be approved by CSRC. While a registration-based mechanism applies to the issuance of commercial paper and medium-term notes, whose issuer provides information about the bond and registers with the National Association of Financial Market Institutional Investors (NAFMII).

and Reform Commission (NDRC), which supervises activities in sectors of the real economy. Further, corporate bonds and asset-backed securities are regulated by the China Securities Regulatory Commission (CSRC).

One critical aspect of green bond regulation is the definition of green assets and projects. Multiple "catalogues" (or taxonomies) were initially developed to support the PRC's overarching green development agenda as the CBIRC, PBOC, and NDRC developed their respective policies, regulations, and instruments. The NDRC published the *Green Industry Guiding Catalogue* in 2019, with the goal of defining the scope of green industry sectors across the economy. The relevant authorities can formulate policies regarding investment, pricing, budgets, and taxation to facilitate the development of green industries based on the industry catalogue and its associated technical criteria instruction document.

The PBOC, the NDRC, and the CSRC released the *Green Bond Endorsed Project Catalogue (2021 Edition)* in April 2021, and it went into effect in July 2021. The 2021 edition's logic and framework, as well as its primary contents, are consistent with and complementary to the *Green Industry Guidance Catalogue (2019 Edition)*.

The *Green Bond Endorsed Project Catalogue (2021 Edition)* brought disparate green bond standards in the PRC under one roof. It covers all types of domestic green bonds—green financial bonds, green enterprise bonds, green corporate bonds, green debt financing instruments, and green asset-backed securities (ABS)—putting an end to ununified green bond standards and facilitating the PRC's green bond market's continued development.

The *Green Bond Endorsed Project Catalogue* (2021 Edition) conforms to international standards. It eliminates sectors relating to the clean use of fossil fuels, which benefits both international investors and the PRC's international influence and convening power on green bond standards (Figure 15).

Figure 15: Timeline of the People's Republic of China's Key Green Bond Policies

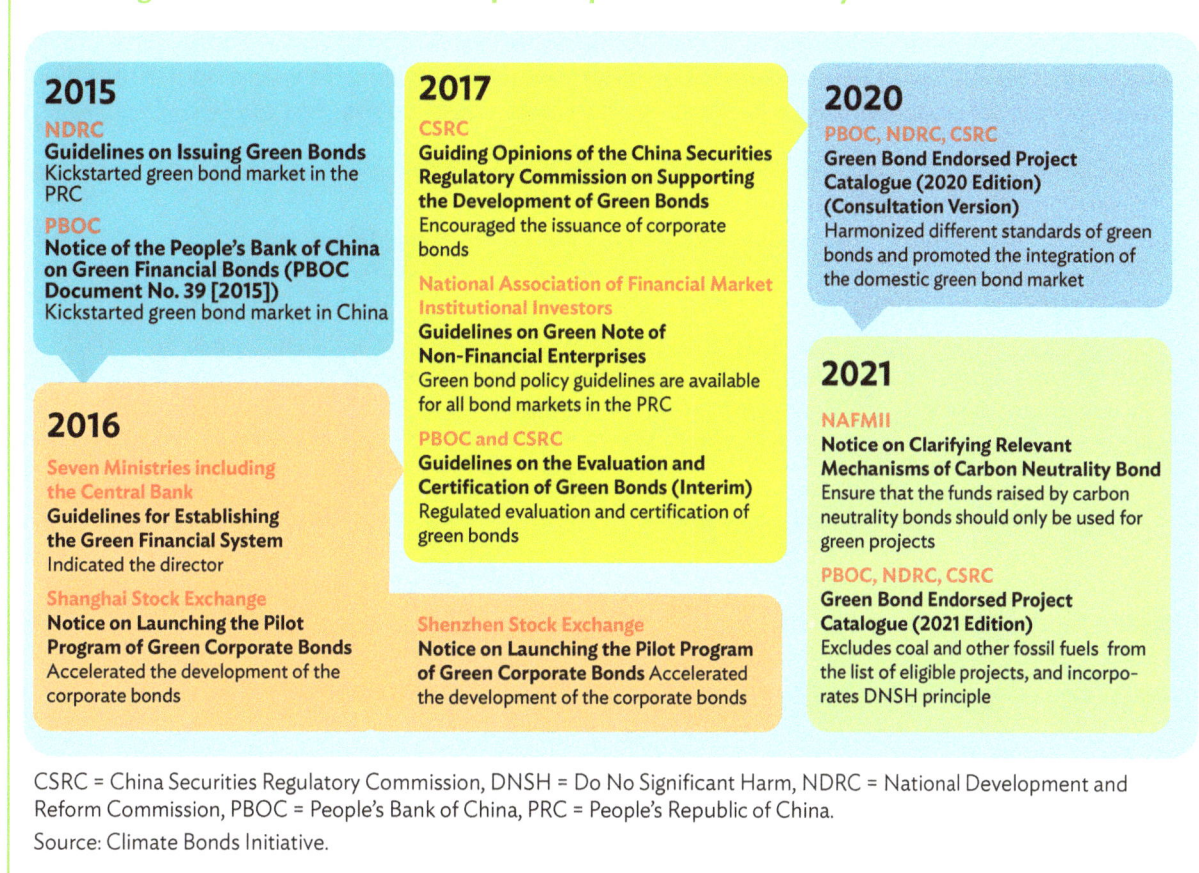

2015

NDRC
Guidelines on Issuing Green Bonds
Kickstarted green bond market in the PRC

PBOC
Notice of the People's Bank of China on Green Financial Bonds (PBOC Document No. 39 [2015])
Kickstarted green bond market in China

2016

Seven Ministries including the Central Bank
Guidelines for Establishing the Green Financial System
Indicated the director

Shanghai Stock Exchange
Notice on Launching the Pilot Program of Green Corporate Bonds
Accelerated the development of the corporate bonds

2017

CSRC
Guiding Opinions of the China Securities Regulatory Commission on Supporting the Development of Green Bonds
Encouraged the issuance of corporate bonds

National Association of Financial Market Institutional Investors
Guidelines on Green Note of Non-Financial Enterprises
Green bond policy guidelines are available for all bond markets in the PRC

PBOC and CSRC
Guidelines on the Evaluation and Certification of Green Bonds (Interim)
Regulated evaluation and certification of green bonds

Shenzhen Stock Exchange
Notice on Launching the Pilot Program of Green Corporate Bonds Accelerated the development of the corporate bonds

2020

PBOC, NDRC, CSRC
Green Bond Endorsed Project Catalogue (2020 Edition) (Consultation Version)
Harmonized different standards of green bonds and promoted the integration of the domestic green bond market

2021

NAFMII
Notice on Clarifying Relevant Mechanisms of Carbon Neutrality Bond
Ensure that the funds raised by carbon neutrality bonds should only be used for green projects

PBOC, NDRC, CSRC
Green Bond Endorsed Project Catalogue (2021 Edition)
Excludes coal and other fossil fuels from the list of eligible projects, and incorporates DNSH principle

CSRC = China Securities Regulatory Commission, DNSH = Do No Significant Harm, NDRC = National Development and Reform Commission, PBOC = People's Bank of China, PRC = People's Republic of China.
Source: Climate Bonds Initiative.

Top policymakers and regulators in the PRC have stepped up their efforts to encourage market participants to consider environmental, social, and climate factors when making investment decisions. Climate Bonds' report, *China's Growing Sustainable Debt Market,* identified a number of noteworthy policy developments, some of which are discussed below.[33]

Financial Support to Prevent and Control the Pandemic

The PBOC, Ministry of Finance, CBIRC, CSRC, and Ministry of Foreign Exchange jointly issued the *Notice on Further Strengthening Financial Support to Prevent and Control the Pandemic* in January 2020, establishing a "fast registration route" for bonds whose proceeds are used for pandemic control. If the issuer is registered or operates in a region severely affected by COVID-19, and/or if the issuer operates in an industry that is either affected by COVID-19 or can contribute to pandemic control, the bond may be labeled "pandemic prevention and control."

CBIRC-Issued Requirements for ESG Risk Management

The CBIRC-issued *Guiding Opinions on Promoting the High-Quality Development of the Banking and Insurance Industry* in January 2020, which sets higher standards for ESG risk management among Chinese financial institutions.

The opinions state clear requirements for banking financial institutions to (i) put in place a sound environmental and social risk management system and incorporate ESG factors into the credit granting process, (ii) encourage the establishment of green finance departments and green branches, and (iii) encourage the development of green financial product innovation.

The Green Financial Performance Evaluation Plan for Banking Depository Financial Institutions includes green bonds.

The PBOC published the *Notice on Releasing the Green Financial Performance Evaluation Plan of Banking Depository Financial Institutions (Draft for Solicitation of Opinions)* in July 2020. This draft revised three sections of the PBOC's *Green Loan Performance Evaluation Plan for Banking Depository Financial Institutions (Trial):*

(i)   the expanded evaluation scope covers not only green loans but also green bonds, with additional room reserved for further incorporation of green equity and green trust;
(ii)   evaluation indicators were revised accordingly based on the expanded scope; and
(iii) the evaluation results can be applied in more scenarios (e.g., it will be referenced by the central bank in the ratings of financial institutions).

The *Green Finance Performance Evaluation Plan for Banking Financial Institutions* was officially released in June 2021. Financial institutions' green bond holdings are explicitly included in the evaluation alongside green credit balances and given the same weighting.

The Shanghai Stock Exchange announced a new regulation on green company bonds.

The Shanghai Stock Exchange issued the *No. 2 Guidelines for the Application of the Review Rules for the Issuance and Listing of Corporate Bonds-Specific Types of Corporate Bonds* in November 2020, which includes regulatory standards, information disclosure, and verification requirements for six different types of bonds: short-term company bonds, renewable bonds, green company bonds, poverty alleviation bonds, innovation bonds, and disaster relief bonds.[34]

---

[33]   Climate Bonds Initiative and CIB Economic Research and Consulting Co., Ltd. 2022. *China's Growing Sustainable Debt Market: Rapid Growth Delivers Impacts.* https://www.climatebonds.net/files/reports/cbi_chi_sust_debt_stock.pdf.

[34]   SSE. 2020. *Notice on the Issuance of the Shanghai Stock Exchange No. 2 Guidelines for the Application of the Review Rules for the Issuance and Listing of Corporate Bonds-Specific Types of Corporate Bonds.* http://www.sse.com.cn/lawandrules/sserules/main/issue/c/c_20201127_5268003.shtml.

The guidelines stipulate that at least 70% of funds raised from green company bonds be used in green projects, and they also include additional information disclosure requirements, such as environmental benefit targets.

Five ministries are promoting climate investment and financing.

The *Guiding Opinions on Promoting Climate Investment and Financing* were issued in October 2020 by five ministries, led by the Ministry of Ecology and Environment. The opinions sought to create a policy environment that encourages climate investment and financing, establishing climate investment and financing standards, and launching local pilot programs.

The CSRC includes ESG information in listed firms' investor relations management.

The CSRC released a consultation draft of its *Investor Relations Management Guidelines for Listed Companies* in February 2021.[35] One of the most significant updates is that ESG information is now required, for the first time, in the management of the company's investor relations.

The Ministry of Ecology and Environment launches public consultation on the national emissions trading scheme draft law.

The Ministry of Ecology and Environment released draft national emissions trading scheme (ETS) legislation for public comment in March 2021.[36] The *Interim Regulations for the Management of Carbon Emissions Trading* refine the existing measures and move the regulations one notch higher within the PRC's legal hierarchy. The draft law connects a national ETS to peak carbon emissions and carbon neutrality targets for the first time.[37]

In September 2021, the Ministry of Ecology and Environment released the draft administrative measures on the disclosure of companies' environmental information (version for public comments), requiring enterprises to disclose environmental information, which includes GHG emissions.[38]

At the COP26, the International Platform on Sustainable Finance published the *Instruction Report and Table for the Proposed Common Ground Taxonomy for Comparing the EU and the PRC.*[39] Version 1 of the Common Ground Taxonomy would further improve the comparability, consistency, and interoperability of sustainable finance standards globally.

In November 2021, the PBOC officially unveiled its green monetary policy tool to support the development of low-carbon sectors (i.e., clean energy, energy efficiency, and low-carbon technology). The interest rate was set at 1.75%, compared to the 3.0%–4.0% market rate. (The rate for midterm lending facility is currently 2.95%.) More stringent disclosure, reporting, and external review provided by third-party verifiers was also required.[40]

[35] CSRC. 2021. *Guidelines for Investor Relations Management of Listed Companies (Draft for Solicitation of Comments).* http://www.csrc.gov.cn/pub/zjhpublic/zjh/202102/t20210205_392304.htm.

[36] Government of the PRC, Ministry of Ecology and Environment. 2021. *Interim Regulations for the Management of Carbon Emissions Trading.* http://www.mee.gov.cn/xxgk2018/xxgk/xxgk06/202103/t20210330_826642.html.

[37] International Carbon Action Partnership. 2021. *China Publishes New Draft National ETS Legislation.* https://icapcarbonaction.com/fr/news-archive/766-china-publishes-new-draft-national-ets-legislation.

[38] Government of the PRC, Ministry of Ecology and Environment. 2021. *Draft Administrative Measures on the Closure of Company's Environmental Information (version for public comments).* https://www.mee.gov.cn/ywgz/zcghtjdd/sthjzc/202109/t20210924_953309.shtml

[39] European Commission. International Platform on Sustainable Finance. https://ec.europa.eu/info/business-economy-euro/banking-and-finance/sustainable-finance/international-platform-sustainable-finance_en.

[40] PBOC. 2021. *The People's Bank of China Launches Carbon Reduction Support Tools.* http://www.pbc.gov.cn/goutongjiaoliu/113456/113469/4384182/index.html.

Policy Incentives and Constraints

Domestic

Green bond investment was included in the PBOC's evaluation of green financial performance, and the results of the evaluation will be incorporated into the central bank's rating of financial institutions. Green loans and green bonds were also added to the list of eligible collateral for monetary policy operations. Green bond investment has been included in the CBIRC's green financing statistics, and the Shanghai Clearing House has reduced the fees and rates charged for green bonds.

Green Bond-Related Policy Incentives and Constraints Set by the PBOC

In June 2018, the central bank decided to appropriately expand the scope of medium-term lending facilities collateral to include green financial bonds, AA+, and AA-rated corporate bonds (priority will be given to bonds involving small and micro enterprises and the green economy), as well as high-quality green loans, in order to expand the scope of eligible collateral for monetary policy operations. This move is expected to increase the market attractiveness of green bonds, encouraging more banks to issue green financial bonds and resulting in more green loans and financial support for green projects and businesses.

In June 2021, the PBOC issued a new Green Financial Evaluation Program for Banking Financial Institutions, which took effect on 1 July 2021 and will be conducted every quarter. The program modifies the PBOC's Green Credit Performance Evaluation Scheme for Depository Financial Institutions in the Banking Sector (Trial), with one of the most significant changes being the addition of green bond assessments. The program proposes that "the results of green financial performance evaluation will be incorporated into the PBOC policy and prudential management tools, such as the central bank's rating of financial institutions."

Green Bond-Related Policy Incentives Set by the CBIRC

As an updated version of the original green credit statistical system, the CBIRC released its latest Green Financing Statistical System in July 2020. The Green Financing Statistical System includes bank green bond investments in addition to statistics on green credit. The system excludes green financial bonds and green credit ABS products when counting the holdings of nonfinancial green bonds invested by banks' own funds (referring to the PBOC's *Green Bond Endorsed Project Catalogue*).

Green Bond Policy Incentives Set by Shanghai Clearing House

The Shanghai Clearing House issued a *Notice on the Reduction of Bond Business Charges* in January 2020, announcing its decision to lower its bond business charges. The issuance and registration fee rate, as well as the services fee for interest payment on green bonds, have been reduced by 50% to support the sustainable development of the green industry.

Local Level

Local governments in the PRC have continued to introduce green bond-supporting policies, moving away from encouragement and toward providing incentive such as interest discounts, guarantees, and green bond subsidies.

One example of a policy that discounts the interest of ABS and green bonds in environmental infrastructure is Jiangsu Province's Implementation Opinions on Deepening Green Financial Services for the High-Quality Development of the Ecological Environment. The interest discount on green bonds, such as Yangtze River Ecological Restoration Bonds, is 30% of the actual annual payment over a 2-year period. The annual subsidy for a single green bond is limited to CNY2 million. The incentives have helped Jiangsu to increase the issuance of green bonds.

In addition to Jiangsu Province's implementation opinions, several governments, including those in the Green Finance Pilot Zones in Sichuan Province and Nanning City in Guangxi Province, have implemented significant incentives such as subsidies for green bond issuers.

Japan

The Government of Japan is designing a green growth strategy with policies for incentivizing green innovation and investments and regulatory reforms favoring clean energy. In October 2020, Japan announced its commitment to net-zero emissions by 2050.[41] This represents a key milestone for the country that aligns its climate ambition with that of the United Kingdom (UK) and other European countries. Japan is also a group of three East Asian countries—accompanying the Republic of Korea and the PRC—to formally commit to net-zero targets.

To achieve carbon neutrality, the Ministry of Economy, Trade and Industry (METI) published *a Green Growth Strategy* in December 2020. The strategy establishes an action plan for 14 priority areas aimed at increasing green power production. The latter includes the development of hydrogen as an energy source and the expansion of offshore wind power generation to generate approximately USD2 trillion in annual green growth.

The Expert Panel on Sustainable Finance was established by the Financial Services Agency (FSA) to encourage domestic and foreign investment in Japanese companies to assist in their transition to carbon neutrality. Representatives from business, finance, and academia, as well as officials from relevant ministries and agencies, make up the panel.

METI also plans to phase out new gasoline-powered vehicles by 2030 to achieve carbon neutrality, implying government support for electrification of road transport. The establishment of market development task forces, the intention to increase green finance, and the recognition and proper management of climate-related risks are all examples of Japan's climate commitment.

Improving Climate Data

The Japan Exchange Group and the Tokyo Stock Exchange jointly published the Practical Handbook for ESG Disclosure in March 2020 to establish standards for listed companies' ESG reporting practices. The handbook identifies potential roadblocks to voluntary ESG disclosure and suggests solutions and processes for overcoming them.[42]

Businesses have been under increasing pressure in recent years to account for and report on their environmental impacts. In Japan, a record number of companies have agreed to report in accordance with recommendations of the Taskforce on Climate-Related Financial Disclosures (TCFD). This significant development is due in part to the establishment of the Japan TCFD Consortium, a public–private partnership supported by the Ministry of the Environment, METI, and the FSA that fosters dialogue and collaboration among organizations to improve their climate-related financial disclosures.

Management of Systemic and Monetary Climate Risk

The FSA and the Bank of Japan have joined the Network for Greening the Financial System to assess and address the risks that climate change poses to the Japanese financial system. The Bank of Japan held an international research workshop on climate-related financial risks in support of this commitment, while the FSA is conducting climate stress tests on the country's major financial institutions.

---

41   Climate Bonds Initiative. Japan: Green Finance State of the Market 2020. https://www.climatebonds.net/resources/reports/japan-green-finance-state-market-2020.

42   World Federation of Exchanges. 2020. Japan Exchange Group and Tokyo Stock Exchange publish ESG disclosure handbook. https://focus.world-exchanges.org/articles/japan-esg-disclosure.

Market Development

The Green Finance Portal was created to provide support and education to green finance stakeholders, such as issuers and investors, on the most recent market developments. In addition, a new subsidy scheme has been established to encourage the issuance of green loans and bonds for adaptation projects. The Financial Support Program for Green Bond Issuance, which began in 2018, continues to provide subsidies for green labeled bond issuance.

To set the process for structuring SLLs, the Ministry of the Environment released the *Green Loan and Sustainability Linked Loan Guidelines* in March 2020 to promote best practices and establish benchmarks for companies that issue such instruments.

Republic of Korea

As referenced in Climate Bonds' market overview report, the Republic of Korea has been active in implementing climate mitigation policy (footnote 41). The country became Asia's first economy to implement an ETS in 2015. There was unwavering support for the Korean ETS bill, which was passed by the Korean Parliament on 2 May 2012 with a 148–0 vote. The Korean Green Growth Act was legislated in 2009 and acts as the legal foundation for the ETS. The Korean ETS is now the world's second largest after the EU ETS and one of only a few that operate fully at the national level.

Foreign Exchange Stabilization Bonds

As part of its Foreign Exchange Stabilization Bonds program, the Government of the Republic of Korea issued a USD500 million sovereign sustainability bond in 2019 to finance projects as defined by the country's Green and Sustainability Bond Framework.[43] This framework[44] is aligned with ICMA's Green, Social, and Sustainability Bond Principles, with proceeds allocated by the Korea Investment Corporation.[45] Further afield, the government is set for a 2021 pilot of a K-taxonomy to define environmentally sustainable industries and economic activities. The Financial Services Commission (FSC) will also introduce best practice guidelines on green finance and climate risk management alongside mandatory ESG disclosure requirements for large companies from 2026 and all listed firms from 2030.[46]

Taxonomy Development

As stated, the Government of the Republic of Korea is set to establish a K-taxonomy to define environmentally sustainable industries and economic activities (footnote 46). When the taxonomy is published, state-backed financial institutions will double green investment from 6.5% to 13.0% of total investments.

Green Capital Market Regulation

The FSC is introducing mandatory ESG disclosure requirements for large companies from 2026 and all listed firms from 2030 (footnote 46).

---

[43]　Government of the Republic of Korea, Securities and Exchange Commission. 2019. Form 424B2 Republic of Korea. https://sec.report/Document/0001193125-19-173021/#supptoc738119_102.

[44]　Sustainalytics. Republic of Korea Green and Sustainability Bond Second Party Opinion. https://www.sustainalytics.com/corporate-solutions/sustainable-finance-and-lending/published-projects/project/republic-of-korea/republic-of-korea-green-and-sustainability-bond-second-party-opinion/republic-of-korea-green-and-sustainability-bond-second-party-opinion-pdf.

[45]　Korea Investment Corporation. 2020. Sustainable Investment Report. https://www.ifswf.org/sites/default/files/annual-reports/KIC_Sustainable_Investment_Report_2020_EN.pdf.

[46]　Financial Services Commission. Green Finance. https://www.fsc.go.kr/eng/po060101.

Green Capital Market Support

The FSC chairs a public–private joint task force on green finance launched in 2020. The task force will create green finance units within state-backed financial institutions. A green finance consultative body launched in May 2021 will formulate an integrated and coordinated framework for the Republic of Korea's green finance strategies and promote information sharing among relevant authorities (footnote 46).

Wider Green Policy Development

The Republic of Korea's Green New Deal aims to support recovery from the pandemic and meet the country's 2050 net-zero goals. Green funding makes up 16% of total stimulus spending (USD48 billion) and includes a public–private green lending facility.[47] The Republic of Korea has a 2050 carbon neutrality target, and its updated Nationally Determined Contribution has an absolute emissions target of a 24.4% reduction by 2030 (compared to 2017).[48] This target has been incorporated into the Third Basic Plan for the K-ETS, 2021– 2030. Korea's ETS currently covers 73.5% of domestic GHG emissions and the plan specifies that the target should be considered when setting emissions cap and allocating permits.

ASEAN Country Developments

Since the late 1980s, ASEAN countries—including Malaysia, Thailand, Singapore, the Philippines, and Viet Nam—have been proactively developing their financial markets to support various national objectives, such as providing high-quality infrastructure and transforming themselves into becoming high-income countries (footnote 17). They have also achieved remarkable progress in developing their respective domestic bond markets.[49] Built on this success, a sustainable finance market has emerged and thrived in Southeast Asia over the past few years. However, it is still at the very nascent stage.

Malaysia

Following its three master plans—the Capital Market Master Plan 1, 2001–2010; Capital Market Master Plan 2, 2010–2020; and the Financial Sector Master Plan, 2001–2010—Malaysia has successfully shored up its weakened banking industry to enhance of its domestic capital market.[50,51] As a result, Malaysia now has a well-balanced onshore bond market that contributes to alleviating currency and maturity mismatches in financing, diversifying credit risks, and facilitating the use of high domestic savings to finance the real economy.

Malaysia has been continually active in the fight against climate change and the pursuit of its SDGs. The government has implemented various initiatives to promote green finance through domestic bank lending equity and fixed-income markets to support the green growth strategy emphasized in its Mid-Term Review of the 11th Malaysia Plan released in October 2018.[52]

---

[47]   Government of the Republic of Korea, Ministry of Economy and Finance. 2020. Government Releases an English Booklet on the Korean New Deal. Press release. 28 July. https://english.moef.go.kr/pc/selectTbPressCenterDtl.do?boardCd=N0001&seq=4948.

[48]   See https://www4.unfccc.int/sites/ndcstaging/PublishedDocuments/Republic%20of%20Korea%20First/211223_The%20Republic%20of%20Korea%27s%20Enhanced%20Update%20of%20its%20First%20Nationally%20Determined%20Contribution_211227_editorial%20change.pdf.

[49]   ADB. 2019. *Good Practices for Developing a Local Currency Bond Market: Lessons from the ASEAN+3 Asian Bond Markets Initiative.* Manila. https://www.think-asia.org/bitstream/handle/11540/10179/developing-lcy-bond-market.pdf?sequence=1.

[50]   Securities Commission Malaysia. Capital Market Masterplan 1. https://www.sc.com.my/resources/publications-and-research/capital-market-masterplan-1.

[51]   Securities Commission Malaysia. Capital Market Masterplan 2. https://www.sc.com.my/resources/publications-and-research/cmp2.

[52]   Securities Commission Malaysia. 2019. *Islamic Green Finance: Development, Ecosystem, and Prospects.* Kuala Lumpur. https://www.sc.com.my/api/documentms/download.ashx?id=a86707ce-07e0-4c75-9e45-7ad7bca6f540.

Green Bonds for Long-Term Financing

In 2014, the Securities Commission Malaysia (SCM) introduced its Sustainable Responsible Investment (SRI) Sukuk Framework, which features guidelines and standards on GSS *sukuk*.[53] The four key components of the framework, which are largely in line with the ICMA's Green Bond Principles (GBP), are (i) use-of-proceeds (UOP), (ii) process for project evaluation and selection, (iii) management of proceeds, and (iv) reporting. In 2019, the SRI Sukuk Framework was revised to enhance the disclosure standards and reporting requirements, as well as to emphasize the role of external reviews in the issuance process, making the framework more convergent to the internationally accepted principles and best practices.[54] Furthermore, the revised framework also expands the list of eligible projects to 10 green and six social categories, a combination of green and social projects and *waqf* (charitable endowment) projects.[55] As such, the SRI Sukuk Framework has played a pivotal role in the creation of an ecosystem that promotes domestic sustainable and responsible investing in Malaysia.

The SCM has offered several incentives to green issuers to complement the framework and stimulate green SRI *sukuk* issuance. Malaysia demonstrated global leadership in 2018 by establishing the Green SRI Sukuk Grant Scheme, which was one of the first incentive structures to support green bond issuance. Green *sukuk* issuers can benefit from tax exemptions. The SRI Sukuk and Bond Grant Scheme was renamed in January 2021, and it now applies to all *sukuk* issued under the SRI Sukuk Framework or bonds issued under the ASEAN Green, Social, and Sustainability Bond Standards (ASEAN Standards).[56] Eligible issuers can use the grant to offset up to 90% of the costs of external review, up to a maximum of MYR300,000 per issuance. Furthermore, the grant's tax exemption was extended for another 5 years until 2025. Meanwhile, until the end of 2023, the existing tax reduction on issuance costs of SRI *sukuk* approved by or lodged with the SCM has been extended. The financial support the grant offers has encouraged more companies to fund GSS projects through SRI *sukuk* and bond issuance.

Malaysia was also the first country in ASEAN to issue sustainable *sukuk* in 2014 and green *sukuk* in 2017, bolstering the country's position as a sustainable Islamic finance hub.[57] Except for the USD680 million sustainability deal by CIMB Bank Berhad and the USD800 million sovereign sustainability bond, almost all GSS bonds and *sukuk* deals have been issued in Malaysian ringgit, with USD-equivalent sizes ranging from about USD30 million to USD500 million, and having longer terms. With 85 % of outstanding GSS bonds offered as *sukuk*, the Malaysian bond market may be mature enough to support the development of a local GSS bond market and serve as a potential hub for GSS Islamic transactions.[58,59]

[53] Securities Commission Malaysia. 2014. SC introduces sustainable and responsible investment *sukuk* framework. News release. 28 August. https://www.sc.com.my/resources/media/media-release/sc-introduces-sustainable-and-responsible-investment-sukuk-framework.

[54] Securities Commission Malaysia. 2019. Sustainable and Responsible Investment Sukuk Framework: An Overview. https://www.sc.com.my/api/documentms/download.ashx?id=84491531-2b7e-4362-bafb-83bb33b07416.

[55] *Waqf* is an Arabic word meaning assets that are donated, bequeathed, or purchased for being held in perpetual trust for general or specific charitable causes that are socially beneficial.

[56] Securities Commission Malaysia. 2021. SRI sukuk and bond grant scheme to encourage capital market fund raising for sustainable development. News release. 21 January. https://www.sc.com.my/resources/media/media-release/sri-sukuk-and-bond-grant-scheme-to-encourage-capital-market-fund-raising-for-sustainable-development.

[57] Malaysian Sustainable Finance Initiative. Sustainable Finance: State of Market in Malaysia. https://www.msfi.com.my/sustainable-finance-state-of-market-in-malaysia.

[58] Climate Bonds Initiative. 2021. *ASEAN Sustainable Finance: State of the Market 2020*. https://www.climatebonds.net/files/reports/asean-sotm-2020.pdf.

[59] Climate Bonds Initiative. 2021. Green Infrastructure Investment Opportunities: Malaysia 2020 Report. https://www.climatebonds.net/files/reports/cbi_giio_malaysia_20_03_bbd.pdf.

Green Index

In 2014, Bursa Malaysia and the FTSE Russell launched an ESG index, the FTSE4Good Bursa Malaysia Index, for the Malaysian market.[60] The index constituents are selected from the top 200 Malaysian stocks in the FTSE Bursa Malaysia EMAS Index based on their ESG performance.[61]

Green Technology Financing Scheme and Financial Institutions' Participation

The Green Technology Financing Scheme (GTFS) is a one-of-a-kind example of how governments can help green projects grow by making financing more accessible and at lower costs.[62] The first version was launched in 2010 with a total target financing approval of MYR3.5 billion (USD750 million).[63] In March 2019, the Ministry of Finance approved an extension of the scheme, known as GTFS 2.0, with an allocation of MYR2 billion (USD500 million) until 2020.[64] The most recent version, GTFS 3.0, has a fund size of MYR2 billion (USD500 million) for 2 years until 2022, with a Danjamin Nasional guarantee to encourage SRI *sukuk* issuances. Green investors benefit from a 2% interest rebate (or the profit rate charged by financial institutions) and a 60% government guarantee on financing provided by financial institutions under the GTFS.[65]

Since its introduction, GTFS has benefited from a great number of green projects (Figure 16), which has led to the creation of 5,000 green jobs and savings of 3,784 million tons of carbon dioxide emissions each year (footnote 63). It has also resulted in the participation of 28 banks and financial institutions with approximately USD875 million in

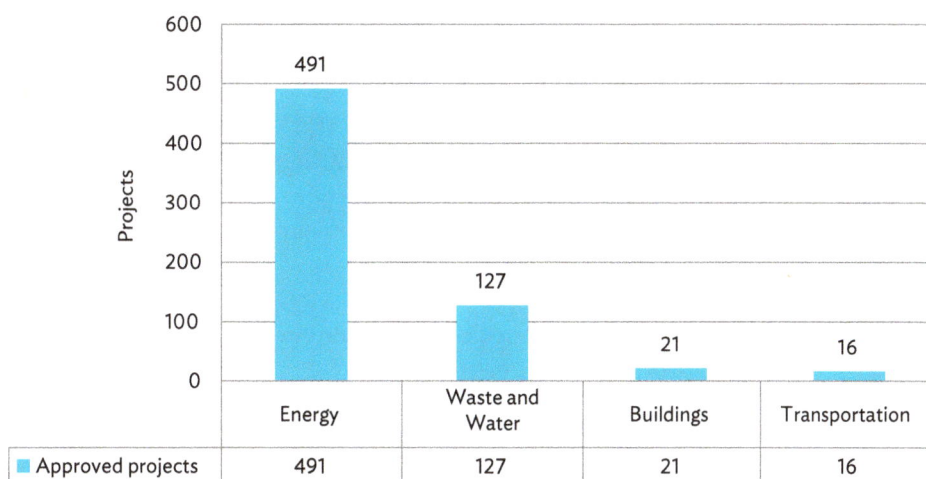

Figure 16: Green Technology Financing Scheme Performance by Sector, 2010–2020

	Energy	Waste and Water	Buildings	Transportation
Approved projects	491	127	21	16

Source: Green Tech Malaysia.

60   Bursa Malaysia. 2018. FTSE4Good Bursa Malaysia Index. 16 March. https://bursasustain.bursamalaysia.com/droplet-details/resources/ftse4good-bursa-malaysia-index
61   Malaysian Sustainable Finance Initiative. FTSE4Good Bursa Malaysia Index. https://www.msfi.com.my/initiatives-ftse4good-bursa-malaysia-index.
62   Bond + Sukuk Information Exchange (BIX). 2021. Advancing Sustainable Finance in Malaysia – the Year in Review. 25 February. https://www.bixmalaysia.com/learning-center/articles-tutorials/advancing-sustainable-finance-in-malaysia.
63   K. I. Jamaludin. Green Technology Financing Facility (GTFS and GTFS 2.0). Presentation. https://www.myhijau.my/wp-content/uploads/2019/04/Slide-Presentation-GTFSv2-Business-Clinic-2019-compressed.pdf.
64   Malaysian Sustainable Finance Initiative. Green Technology Financing Scheme (GTFS). https://www.msfi.com.my/incentives-green-technology-financing-scheme-gtfs.
65   GreenTech Malaysia. Green Technology Financing Facility (GTFS and GTFS 2.0). https://www.myhijau.my/wp-content/uploads/2019/04/Slide-Presentation-GTFSv2-Business-Clinic-2019-compressed.pdf.

loans as of July 2018.[66] Of all projects financed, about 53% came from conventional finance, with the rest funded by Islamic sources.[67]

Taxonomy Development

On 30 April 2021, Bank Negara Malaysia released its Climate Change and Principle-Based Taxonomy (CCPT) as the guiding principles related to climate objectives for financial institutions and other market players.[68] The primary objective is to provide a standardized classification and reporting of climate-related exposures, and to support risk assessments and monitoring of their financing and investments. Although the CCPT does not distinguish its application between the retail and corporate segments, it is more corporate-focused given that corporate segments have a comparatively higher carbon footprint.[69]

In December 2021, the SCM released its consultation paper on its principles-based SRI Taxonomy.[70] The SRI Taxonomy was developed to enable capital market participants to identify economic activities that align with environmental, social, and sustainability objectives, and provide guiding principles in financing a credible transition.

At present, Malaysia is relatively more advanced compared to other neighboring countries in terms of providing necessary prerequisites for the GSS bond market development, ranging from a well-developed domestic bond market to supporting policies and incentives and a standardized taxonomy. However, the LCY GSS bond market remains relatively microscopic. The lack of viable and investment-ready projects suggests a need for greater visibility of green infrastructure investment pipelines. These pipelines could help investors understand that there is a sufficiently large pool of financially attractive investments that are also green. Additionally, the government also should consider issuing a sovereign or sub-sovereign green bond to send a strong signal to the market and help it grow.

Thailand

Thailand has made concerted efforts to develop its LCY bond market by adopting successive capital market master plans. The Thai bond market has grown rapidly in the aftermath of the 1997/98 Asian financial crisis and is the second-largest among all ASEAN bond markets (after Malaysia) with annual average growth of 10% since 2010.[71] The Thai bond market is dominated by government bonds that have seen consistent growth over the years, reaching THB6 trillion (USD175 billion) in 2020. Corporate bond volumes remain a fraction of the total value, but they have also developed positively over the last few years (Figure 17).

The comparatively well-developed Thai bond market could facilitate the integration of green bonds into the capital structure if there were enough suitable assets and projects in the real economy. Thailand has achieved some progress on sustainable finance development, with the growing bond market and investor awareness. In August 2020, Thailand issued a sovereign sustainability bond with an initial value of THB30 billion (USD960 million). This has subsequently been reopened multiple times and as of March 2022 stood at THB197 billion (USD6.5 billion). This bond was extremely well received by the capital market and achieved a pricing benefit (greenium).

[66] F. H. Hussain. 2020. Green loans: Financing the transition to a low-carbon economy. *World Bank Blogs.* 27 April. https://blogs.worldbank.org/climatechange/green-loans-financing-transition-low-carbon-economy.

[67] Malaysian Green Technology Corporation. 2019. *Green Technology Financing Facility (GTFS and GTFS 2.0)*. https://www.myhijau.my/wp-content/uploads/2019/04/Slide-Presentation-GTFSv2- Business-Clinic-2019-compressed.pdf.

[68] Bank Negara Malaysia. 2021. *Climate Change and Principle-Based Taxonomy*. 30 April. https://www.bnm.gov.my/documents/20124/938039/Climate+Change+and+Principle-based+Taxonomy.pdf.

[69] Deloitte. 2021. *The Climate Change Principle-based Taxonomy and its implications to Financial Institutions.* https://www2.deloitte.com/content/dam/Deloitte/my/Documents/risk/my-risk-climate-change-principle.pdf.

[70] Securities Commission Malaysia. 2021. SC invites public feedback on sustainable and responsible investment taxonomy. News release. 17 December. https://www.sc.com.my/resources/media/media-release/sc-invites-public-feedback-on-sustainable-and-responsible-investment-taxonomy.

[71] ThaiBMA. About Thai Bond Market. https://www.thaibma.or.th/EN/Education/ThaiBondMarket.aspx.

Figure 17: Value of Outstanding Bonds in the Thai Market
(THB billion)

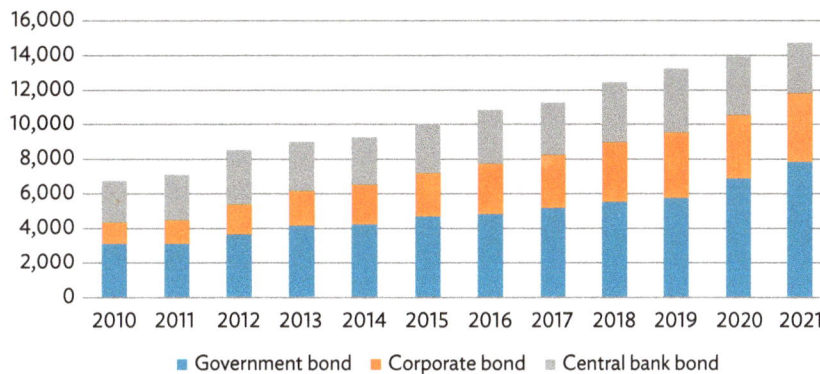

THB = Thai baht.
Source: AsianBondsOnline.

Meanwhile, the Securities and Exchange Commission of Thailand (SEC Thailand) approved the Sustainability Development Roadmap in 2019, incorporating it into the SEC Strategic Plan, 2020–2022.[72] The SEC Strategic Plan, 2021–2023 maintains a goal to build a robust foundation to support sustainable development. The Sustainability Development Roadmap will impact the sustainable development of listed companies and aim at improving the important enablers for the green bond market, including demand, supply, and opportunities and obstacles in the Thai capital market. In the same year, the Bank of Thailand also became a member of the Network of Central Banks and Supervisors for Greening the Financial System.

Most recently, the SEC published the SEC Strategic Plan, 2022–2024, which aims to achieve three main objectives: (i) enhancing competitiveness, (ii) ensuring inclusiveness, and (iii) strengthening trust and confidence in the Thai capital market. Among five key results outlined in the strategic plan, the SEC seeks to strengthen the capital market's capacity for sustainability through the following measures:[73]

Enhancing ESG practices to be on par with international standards:

(i)   promoting carbon neutrality in accordance with Thailand's commitment announced at the Conference of the Parties' World Leaders Summit in Glasgow in November 2021,
(ii)   conducting due diligence with regard to human rights, and
(iii)   promote implementation of the United Nations SDGs among listed companies and relevant capital market stakeholders.

Promoting integration of ESG in business operations:

(i)   issuing environmental risk management guidelines for fund management companies and analysts,
(ii)   issuing guidelines to encourage the incorporation of sustainability considerations into the operations of fund management businesses companies, and
(iii)   organizing capacity-building programs for regulated entities.

---

[72]   Securities and Exchange Commission of Thailand. Sustainability development roadmap: Overview. https://www.sec.or.th/cgthailand/EN/pages/overview/sustainabledevelopmentroadmap.aspx.

[73]   Securities and Exchange Commission of Thailand. 2022. SEC Strategic Plan 2022-2024 aims to revive Thailand toward strength and sustainable growth. News release. 25 March. https://www.sec.or.th/EN/Pages/News_Detail.aspx?SECID=9360.

Green Bonds for Long-Term Financing

GSS finance is growing in Thailand, boosted by the strong economic performance. GSS bonds, including SLBs, originating from Thailand stood at USD5.0 billion (THB154.7 billion) as of the end of Q3 2021. All bonds were issued in Thai baht. The SEC published regulations and guidelines on the issuance and sale of GSS bonds in 2018 and 2019.[74] Issuers are permitted to use any internationally accepted GSS bond standards. The SEC also encourages the appointment of an external reviewer. In case the external reviewer has been appointed, issuers of these thematic bonds are required to disclose the credentials of such reviewers and the scope of review throughout the tenure of the bond. To promote the sustainable development of businesses across multiple industries, SEC Thailand announced regulations in May 2021 governing the issuance and sale of SLBs. The SLB regulations are also based on internationally recognized standards and incorporate references to conventional debt securities regulations.

The issues related to sustainability is one of the key priorities in the SEC strategic plan and several initiatives that contribute to Thailand's sustainable capital market ecosystem have been implemented. In a bid to promote sustainable investment, SEC Thailand has launched the Investment Governance Code containing guidance reflecting internationally accepted standards for responsible investment.

Regulations for disclosure standards of a Sustainable and Responsible Investing Fund (SRI Fund) to widen access for retail investors will also be issued. As external reviews increase investor confidence in the thematic bonds, SEC Thailand has collaborated with a variety of stakeholders, including international organizations, to arrange capacity building programs for potential local external reviewers. Moreover, SEC Thailand and the Thai Bond Market Association (ThaiBMA) have together designed and launched the Sustainable Information Platform to serve as an information center of GSS bonds and SLBs to create the visibility of the sustainability-themed products.

Efforts have also been made to offset the additional monitoring and verification costs associated with issuing GSS bonds. For example, the SEC waived approval and filing fees for green bonds, social bonds, and sustainability bonds issued between May 2019 and May 2022. This incentive was also expanded to include SLBs upon the implementation of the Notification of the Capital Market Supervisory Board Tor Jor. 31/2564 Re: Application and Approval for Offer for Sale of Newly Issued Sustainability-Linked Bonds in May 2021. On 3 March 2022, the SEC's board approved the extension of this incentive through 31 May 2025 and removed restrictions on the UOP from green bonds, social bonds, and sustainability bonds. Previously, the proceeds must be used in Thailand and neighboring countries. This restriction has been removed from the new incentive in favor of promoting business operations that help address global climate change. Similarly, the ThaiBMA announced that the application fee for GSS bonds issued would be waived, in accordance with SEC regulations, and the annual fee would be reduced by THB10,000 per year, effective from 26 March 2019 to 28 June 2020. This incentive was extended until June 2022 and expanded to include SLBs.

In August 2021, the Working Group on Sustainable Finance—comprising representatives from the Fiscal Policy Office, the Bank of Thailand, the SEC, the Office of the Insurance Commission, and the Stock Exchange of Thailand (SET)—released Sustainable Finance Initiatives for Thailand.[75] The initiatives recommend five key strategic initiatives: (i) developing a practical taxonomy, (ii) improving the data environment, (iii) implementing effective incentives, (iv) creating demand-led products and services, and (v) building human capital. As such, it will establish the direction and framework for promoting sustainable finance throughout Thailand's financial sector.

---

[74]   This paragraph refers to the unofficial English translation provided at SEC Thailand. Guidelines on Issuance and Offer for Sale of Green Bond and Sustainability Bond. https://capital.sec.or.th/webapp//nrs/data/7874ae11.pdf. The guidelines in the original Thai language can be accessed at https://capital.sec.or.th/webapp/nrs/data/7874a11.pdf.

[75]   Securities and Exchange Commission of Thailand. *Sustainable Finance Initiatives for Thailand.* https://www.sec.or.th/TH/Documents/KnowledgeBase/SustainableFinanceInitiativesforThailand.pdf.

Green Funds

Thailand has established several funds to support green infrastructure and renewable energy projects in order to foster a pipeline of green assets in the real economy. The Energy Conservation Promotion (ENCON) Fund is a domestic initiative that was established in 1992 under the ENCON Act B.E. 2535 and became operational in 1995.[76] Since its inception, the ENCON fund has served as the government's primary financial vehicle for facilitating the development of renewable energy and energy efficiency in Thailand. Each year the fund raises approximately USD200 million, and it reached total capital of approximately USD1 billion in 2017. The fund has invested in over 1,000 projects.[77] Furthermore, the ENCON fund is also the main funding source for two other successful energy efficiency funding schemes: the Energy Efficiency Revolving Fund and the Energy Service Company Revolving Fund.

The ENCON fund has achieved unprecedented success and demonstrates how governments can foster the growth of green initiatives. The complete methodology for selecting projects is not available, and while it appears to be broadly consistent with the Climate Bonds Taxonomy and Standard, there may be some areas where they diverge (Figure 18).

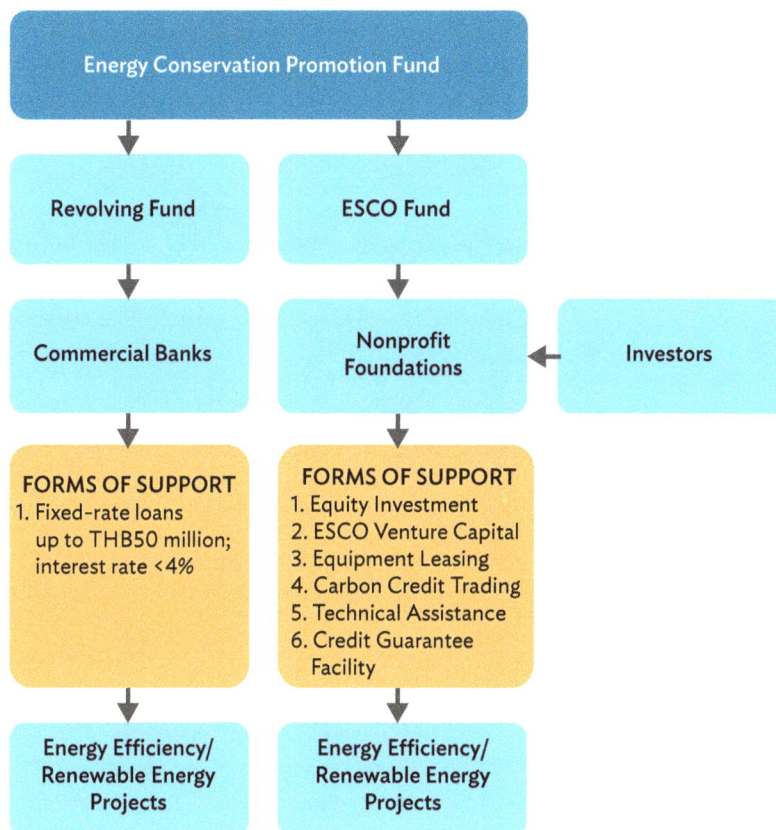

Figure 18: Energy Conservation Promotion Fund Structure

ESCO = energy services company, THB = Thai baht.

Source: Adopted from Asia-Pacific Economic Cooperation. 2021. http://ccap.org/assets/CCAP-Booklet_Thailand.pdf.

---

[76] ASEAN Centre for Energy. 2019. *Energy Efficiency Financing Guideline in Thailand.* https://agep.aseanenergy.org/wp-content/uploads/2019/05/EEF-Guideline-in-Thailand.pdf.

[77] Royal Thai Embassy. Energy Ministry ready to fund 1,000 renewables projects. https://thaiembdc.org/2020/09/11/energy-ministry-ready-to-fund-1000-renewables-projects.

The Energy Efficiency Revolving Fund was launched in 2003 to encourage private investment participation in energy efficiency and renewable energy projects and familiarize banks with financing these types of projects.[78] The fund provided credit lines to local banks which were then able to lend energy efficiency and renewable energy projects project developers with concessional loans. Between 2003 and 2019, the Energy Efficiency Revolving Fund was implemented in seven phases (Table 5).

Table 5: Energy Efficiency Revolving Fund Phases

	Phases 1–5	Phases 6–6+
Time frame	2003–2013	2015–2019
No. of projects funded	295	160
Total funding provided	THB7.2 billion (USD216 million)	THB4.2 billion (USD126.3 million)
Maximum loan size	THB50 million (USD1.6 million)	THB50 million (USD1.5 million)
No. of participating banks	11	8
Interest granted to banks p.a.	0.5%	0%
Interest granted by banks p.a.	Less than 4%	3.5%
Electricity energy savings p.a.	1,170 MWh	12,000 MWh
Total cost savings	THB6.8 billion (USD204 million)	THB512 million (USD15.4 million)

MWh = megawatt-hour, p.a. = per annum, THB = Thai baht, USD = United States dollar.
Source: ASEAN Centre for Energy. 2019. Energy Efficiency Financing Guidelines in Thailand. https://agep.aseanenergy.org/wp-content/uploads/2019/05/EEF-Guideline-in-Thailand.pdf.

Scaling up sustainable investment in the future will be contingent on the Thai government's commitment to greening the economy. Any policies that encourage public investment in green infrastructure have the potential to set Thailand on a long-term sustainable path—sending a critical signal to the market and allowing the country to access new capital. Additionally, any strategies for updating and incorporating international and regional guidelines and best practices into domestic regulations, particularly internationally accepted definitions of green, are necessary to avoid market fragmentation and facilitate international capital flows.

Sustainable Banking

Beyond the achievements of the regulators, leadership has been shown in the banking sector. In 2019, the Thai Bankers' Association (TBA) introduced the Sustainable Banking Guidelines for Responsible Lending with support from the Bank of Thailand.[79] Under the guidelines, Thai banks are encouraged to establish internal policies and processes to address key ESG risks in their lending activities. Thus, the guidelines have set a precedent, highlighting the importance of sustainable banking in translating the nation's reform efforts into a competitive and resilient financial sector. In early 2020, the Association of International Banks in Thailand also adopted the guidelines.

Commercial banks in Thailand have led on green finance by issuing green and sustainability bonds to fund and refinance green assets. To date, the Thai banks that have issued green and sustainability bonds are TMB Bank (now known as TMBThanachart Bank) and Kasikorn Bank for a total amount of USD342 million.[80] Many banks are also providing green loans and other tools for green projects (i.e., renewable energy and energy efficiency). For instance, Bangkok Bank introduced the Bualuang Green Loan program to support small and medium-sized enterprises (SMEs) that invest in environment-friendly businesses through the concept of reuse and recycle, and emit no pollutants. Meanwhile, Kasikorn Bank also launched the K-Energy Saving Guarantee Program that supports

---

[78]   ASEAN Centre for Energy. 2019. *Energy Efficiency Financing Guideline in Thailand*. https://agep.aseanenergy.org/wp-content/uploads/2019/05/EEF-Guideline-in-Thailand.pdf.

[79]   See https://www.tba.or.th/wp-content/uploads/2019/08/Guidelines-ResponsibleLending.pdf.

[80]   According to the CBI database, including the USD100 million sustainability bond from Kasikorn Bank in October 2021.

investment in energy efficiency projects through service from an energy management company. Another example is the SME Go Green scheme initiated by Siam Commercial Bank.[81] The bank agrees to provide green loans to green SMEs to cover their long-term and working capital for clean energy and pollution management, which will help to reduce energy consumption.

Greening the Stock Exchange

Thailand has emerged as a regional leader in ESG disclosures with 100% of listed companies reporting ESG information.[82] In 2015, the SET created the Thailand Sustainability Investment (THSI) list for investors seeking an alternative investment in high-performing ESG stocks while also supporting sustainable Thai businesses. SET defines sustainable businesses as those that balance risk management, supply chain management, and innovation with ESG responsibilities.

To complement the THSI, SET launched the Thailand Sustainability Investment Index in 2018, which consists of high-performing stocks from an ESG standpoint, in order to attract investors interested in the responsible investment trend. Furthermore, Thai listed companies of all sizes will be encouraged to adopt the ESG concept, with the goal of increasing their visibility in global sustainability indices, thereby raising global investor awareness. Through its Sustainable Capital Market Development initiative, the SET also organizes various training programs and provides sustainable business development tools for listed companies to integrate SDGs in their operations.

In September 2020, SEC Thailand amended the regulations on the preparation of the annual registration statement (Form 56-1) and annual report (Form 56-2) by consolidating both forms into one called Form 56-1 One Report. This 56-1 One Report will not only reduce the burden of ongoing reporting of listed firms but also improve the quality of ESG disclosure by requiring the listed firms to disclose more on how their businesses have been operating under the ESG principles. For instance, disclosure of policies, goals, and ESG-oriented performance; GHGs; and respect for human rights. In addition, the registration statement for securities offering of both Thai and foreign firms has also been revised to be in line with the Form 56-1 One Report. The Form 56-1 One Report will come into force for the accounting period ending 31 December 2021 and the revised registration statement is effective from 1 January 2022 onward.

Since December 2020, SEC Thailand has become an official Taskforce on Climate-Related Financial Disclosures (TCFD) supporter.[83] In doing so, it aims to encourage businesses to follow international standard disclosure guidelines and incorporate climate-related risks into their strategic planning and risk management. This is expected to enhance the Thai capital market's capacity for contributing to the sustainable development of the country.

Singapore

Singapore is a developed market with an established presence in global capital markets. Entities located in Singapore can satisfy large-scale borrowing needs in the international capital markets, often achieving efficient funding by borrowing in the major foreign currencies, particularly in US dollars. According to the Monetary Authority of Singapore (MAS), the Singaporean LCY corporate bond market is relatively smaller compared to the foreign currency market. For instance, non-SGD corporate debt issuances accounted for 87.7% (SGD204 billion) of total debt issuances in 2019 and 89.3% (SGD200 billion) in 2020 (Figure 19).[84, 85]

[81]   Siam Commercial Bank. 2020. 'SME Go Green' Loan from SCB lets SMEs go lean and green, while boosting sustainability and a positive economy. News release. https://www.scb.co.th/en/about-us/news/jul-2020/nws-sme-go-green.html.

[82]   M. Senanarong. 2019. ESG and *Responsible Investing in Thailand. Presentation during the ASEAN Institutional Investors Forum.* 14 June. https://www.setsustainability.com/download/jsfgbpi6nzawm8l.

[83]   Securities and Exchange Commission of Thailand. 2021. SEC becomes a supporter of the Task Force on Climate-Related Financial Disclosures (TCFD supporter). News release. 15 January. https://www.sec.or.th/EN/Pages/News_Detail.aspx?SECID=8746&NewsNo=11&NewsYear=2021&Lang=EN.

[84]   Monetary Authority of Singapore. 2020. *Singapore Corporate Debt Market Development 2020.* https://www.mas.gov.sg/-/media/MAS/News-and-Publications/Surveys/Debts/Singapore-Corporate-Debt-Market-Development-2020.pdf.

[85]   Monetary Authority of Singapore. 2021. *Singapore Corporate Debt Market Development 2021.* https://www.mas.gov.sg/-/media/MAS/News-and-Publications/Surveys/Debts/Singapore-Corporate-Debt-Market-Development-2021.pdf.

Figure 19: Singapore's Local Currency Corporate Bond Issuance, 2019 versus 2020

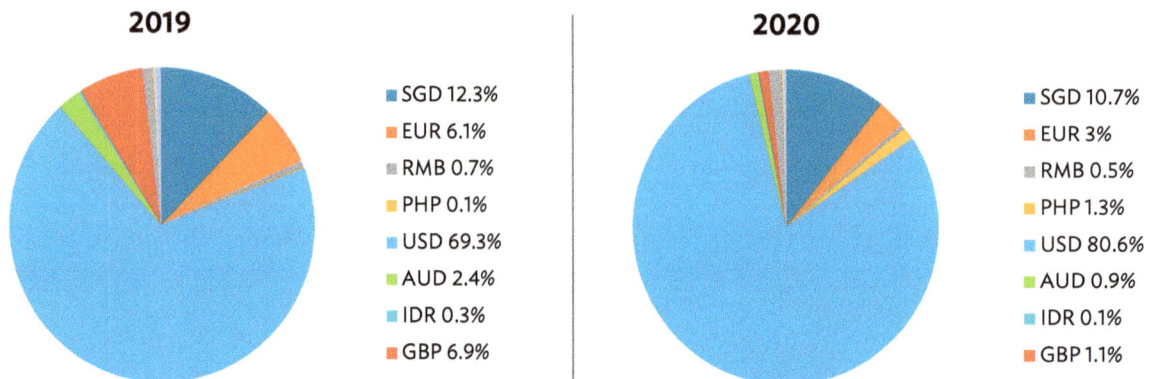

2019

- SGD 12.3%
- EUR 6.1%
- RMB 0.7%
- PHP 0.1%
- USD 69.3%
- AUD 2.4%
- IDR 0.3%
- GBP 6.9%

2020

- SGD 10.7%
- EUR 3%
- RMB 0.5%
- PHP 1.3%
- USD 80.6%
- AUD 0.9%
- IDR 0.1%
- GBP 1.1%

AUD = Australian dollar, EUR = euro, IDR = Indonesian rupiah, PHP = Philippine peso, RMB = Chinese yuan, SGD = Singapore dollar, USD = United States dollar.

Source: Monetary Authority of Singapore. 2020. Singapore Corporate Debt Market Development 2020. https://www.mas.gov.sg/-/media/MAS/News-and-Publications/Surveys/Debts/Singapore-Corporate-Debt-Market-Development-2020.pdf; Monetary Authority of Singapore. 2021. Singapore Corporate Debt Market Development 2021. https://www.mas.gov.sg/-/media/MAS/News-and-Publications/Surveys/Debts/Singapore-Corporate-Debt-Market-Development-2021.pdf?la=en&hash =610BD5E4FCD87E64271B95EAB6E35A828E9E7B16.

The Government of Singapore, through the MAS, has promulgated and implemented core policies and regulatory measures that seek to establish Singapore as a leading center for sustainable finance in Asia and globally.

Green Bonds for Long-Term Financing

Singapore is home to the largest sustainable finance market in ASEAN (footnote 58). To support the evolution of the market, the MAS developed the Green Bond Grant Scheme in June 2017, which was expanded and became the Sustainable Bond Grant Scheme in February 2019.[86] It encourages the issuance of green, social, and sustainability and sustainability-linked bonds in Singapore by funding 100% of eligible expenses attributable to obtaining pre-issuance external review or rating, as well as post-issuance external review or report for up to a grant amount of SGD100,000 for each qualifying issuance. The scheme supports both first-time and repeat issuers, and issuers may apply for the grant each time they have a qualifying issuance.

In November 2019, the MAS released its Green Finance Action Plan, which aims to strengthen the financial sector's resilience to environmental risks, develop green financial solutions, enhance comparability and reliability of sustainability-related disclosures, build knowledge and capabilities in sustainable finance, and leverage innovation and technology.[87] Within the scope of this action plan, the MAS set up a USD2 billion Green Investment Programme to place funds with asset managers committed to growing green capabilities in Singapore. Recognizing the role of the financial sector in addressing the impact of environmental risk and mobilizing capital for the green economy, in 2020, the MAS introduced a set of guidelines that set out supervisory expectations on how financial institutions incorporate environmental risk management in their business operations.[88] The disclosure of environmental risks is also applicable to nonfinancial corporations, which is reflected in Singapore Exchange's requirements that all listed companies produce annual sustainability reports on a comply-or-explain basis.

---

[86] Monetary Authority of Singapore. Sustainable Bond Grant Scheme. https://www.mas.gov.sg/schemes-and-initiatives/sustainable-bond-grant-scheme.

[87] Monetary Authority of Singapore. 2020. Green Finance Action Plan. https://www.mas.gov.sg/-/media/MAS/News/Media-Releases/2020/MAS-Green-Finance-Action-Plan.pdf.

[88] Monetary Authority of Singapore. 2020. MAS Consults on Environmental Risk Management Guidelines for Financial Institutions. News release. 25 June. https://www.mas.gov.sg/news/media-releases/2020/mas-consults-on-environmental-risk-management-guidelines-for-financial-institutions.

In February 2021, Singapore introduced its Singapore Green Plan 2030, a nationwide movement to advance Singapore's national agenda on sustainable development and features five key pillars: (i) city in nature, (ii) sustainable living, (iii) energy reset, (iv) green economy, and (v) resilient future.[89] To achieve these targets, the government will be introducing an array of initiatives, one of which is to develop green finance in the country to the extent that it becomes a global or Asian green finance hub.

Issuance of Green Bonds for Public Infrastructure

The Government of Singapore's statutory boards announced in the 2021 budget that they would issue green bonds to finance selected public infrastructure projects. Public sector green bond issuance is expected to contribute to the development of Singapore's green bond market by attracting green issuers, capital, and investors. By 2030, the Singapore government intends to issue up to SGD35 billion in green bonds to finance public sector green infrastructure projects. The government will establish a framework for sovereign green bond issuances and will collaborate with the statutory boards to support their green bond issuances.

Greening the Stock Exchange

In 2011, the Singapore Exchange (SGX) took the first step by releasing voluntary guidelines for sustainability reporting for listed firms, which was made mandatory in 2016 according to Sustainability Reporting Guidelines on a "comply or explain" basis.[90] The move aims to enhance the visibility of these entities and ensured that they would remain competitive and attractive to investors. Alongside that, to profile Singapore's leaders in ESG standards, SGX also launched a set of four SGX Sustainability Indexes in 2016.

Most recently, in December 2021, SGX introduced several enhancements to its sustainability reporting regime for listed entities with effect from the financial year commencing in 2022. This includes climate reporting consistent with the recommendations of the TCFD for all issuers on a "comply or explain" basis from financial year 2022, and mandatory reporting for issuers in (i) financial; (ii) agriculture, food, and forest products; and (iii) energy industries from financial year 2023; followed by (iv) materials and buildings; and (v) transportation industries from financial year 2024.

Indonesia

In relative terms, Indonesia has a large equity market compared to the size of its banking sector, but a smaller and very fragmented debt securities market. Government bonds represent the bulk of debt securities, with the most denominated in a foreign currency.[91] Foreign investors and banks are the main investors in government bonds, while pension funds, mutual funds, and insurance companies are the main investors in corporate bonds.[92] LCY bonds are not yet a significant source of funding for infrastructure projects, which are primarily financed by large banks and development banks (footnote 92). The government is committed to developing the GSS debt markets and since 2018 has issued four sovereign green *sukuk* instruments with a combined face value of USD3.5 billion.

---

89   Government of Singapore. SG Green Plan. https://www.greenplan.gov.sg.
90   Singapore Exchange. 2016. Practice Note 7.6 Sustainability Reporting Guide. http://rulebook.sgx.com/rulebook/practice-note-76-sustainability-reporting-guide.
91   C. Amariei, W. P. De Groen, and D. Valiente. 2017. *Improving the Investor Base for Local Bond Markets in China, India, and Indonesia. Brussels: Centre for European Policy Studies.* https://www.ceps.eu/wp-content/uploads/2017/10/LocalCurrencyBondMarkets.pdf.
92   Green Finance Platform. 2017. Indonesia's Regulation on the Issuance and the Terms of Green Bond (No. 60/POJK.04/2017) Sets Standards for Green Bond Issuance. https://www.greenfinanceplatform.org/policies-and-regulations/indonesias-regulation-issuance-and-terms-green-bond-no-60pojk042017-sets.

Green Bonds for Long-Term Financing

Indonesia has the second-largest green finance market in the ASEAN region. Indonesia has a comparatively well-developed GSS bond policy framework. For instance, the government developed the Roadmap for Sustainable Finance in Indonesia, 2015–2019 to achieve sustainable development through comprehensive support of the financial service industry. The Financial Services Authority (OJK) also released a regulation on the issuance and terms of green bonds (footnote 92).

Following the implementation of the Roadmap Phase I in 2017, Indonesia launched POJK 51/POJK.03/2017 on the Implementation of Sustainable Finance for Financial Services Companies, Issuers, and Public Companies.[93] The regulation sets out obligations and requirements in implementing sustainable finance for financial institutions, issuers, and public companies, and requires the submission of a sustainable financial action plan and sustainable report to the OJK. The OJK also issued guidelines for securities companies and investment managers to support the implementation of sustainable finance in accordance with the regulation cited above.

Another important policy framework in support of the development of the Indonesian financial market is the National Strategy for Financial Market Development, 2018–2024, which was co-created by the Ministry of Finance, Bank Indonesia, and the OJK.[94] It provides a comprehensive and measurable single policy framework oriented toward creating deep, liquid, efficient, inclusive, and secure financial markets, including the GSS debt market.

In December 2020, the OJK introduced the Indonesian Financial Services Sector Master Plan, 2021–2025 to help overcome the short-term challenges of the COVID-19 pandemic and enhance the resilience and competitiveness in the financial service sector.[95] This master plan builds on its predecessor plan (2015–2019) and focuses on three areas: (i) strengthened resilience and competitiveness, (ii) development of a financial services ecosystem, and (iii) digital transformation acceleration. In recognition that the financial services sector cannot be separated from the need to support sustainable development, the OJK also emphasizes the importance of increasing the role of financial services in sustainable finance to achieve the SDGs in the master plan. To meet this goal, the OJK is preparing an initiative to create a sustainable finance ecosystem in Indonesia, including a sustainable finance taxonomy.

In addition to strengthening the regulatory framework for Indonesia's bond and capital markets, the OJK launched the Sustainable Finance Roadmap Phase II, 2021–2025 on 15 January 2021 to build on the successful implementation of key milestones under Phase I, which ran from 2015 to 2019. The updated Sustainable Finance Roadmap Phase II, 2021–2025 includes plans for the development of a complete market ecosystem for sustainable finance and the definition of an appropriate taxonomy in conjunction with other institutions. It also hopes to address the limited amount of research into sustainable finance and the lack of human resources dedicated to assessing and verifying green and other sustainable finance projects.

To support the implementation of sustainable finance in capital markets as stated in the Roadmap for Sustainable Finance Phase II, 2021–2025, PT Bursa Efek Indonesia (IDX), together with PT Kliring Penjaminan Efek Indonesia (KPEI) and PT Kustodian Sentral Efek Indonesia (KSEI), and supported by the OJK, launched the Environmental, Social, and Governance Platform in the form of an ESG microsite.[96]

---

[93] https://www.ifc.org/wps/wcm/connect/bab66a7c-9dc2-412f-81f6-f83f94d79660/Indonesia+OJK+Sustainable+Finance+Regulation_English. pdf?MOD=AJPERES&CVID=IVXU.Oy.

[94] Bank Indonesia. 2010. *National Strategy for Financial Market Development 2018-2024*. https://www.bi.go.id/en/publikasi/kajian/Documents/ SNPPPK-BI-EN.pdf.

[95] Indonesia Financial Services Authority (OJK). 2020. *The Indonesian Financial Services Sector Master Plan 2021–2025*. Jakarta. https://ojk.go.id/ id/berita-dan-kegiatan/publikasi/Documents/Pages/Master-Plan-Sektor-Jasa-Keuangan-Indonesia-2021-2025/The%20Indonesian%20 Financial%20Services%20Sector%20Master%20Plan%202021-2025.pdf.

[96] Indonesia Capital Market (ESG). https://esg.idx.co.id.

As of December 2021, Indonesia had four local green indexes: (i) SRI KEHATI Index, (ii) IDX ESG Leader Index, (iii) ESG Sector Leaders IDX KEHATI Index, and (iv) ESG Quality 45 IDX KEHATI Index. In 2021, IDX announced support for TCFD and committed to helping Indonesian listed companies implement the TCFD recommendations. Indonesia's four sovereign bonds have added credibility to the efforts that are being made to galvanize a domestic GSS debt market and have earned Indonesia international recognition as a pioneer. Most recently, Indonesia launched the Indonesia Green Taxonomy (Edition 1.0) in January 2022.

Blended Finance and the Sustainable Development Goals

The blended finance model is widely regarded as an innovative method to raise private capital on a global scale. By lowering the entry barriers to private finance through official development assistance and philanthropic funding, the approach helps to de-risk investment.[97]

Indonesia has shown a strong commitment to accelerating the development of sustainable projects by scaling up blended finance. At the United Nations Climate Summit Action in New York in September 2019, the government unveiled the Blended Finance and Innovation Institute. The institute will serve as an ASEAN hub and global accelerator for blended finance geared toward achieving the SDGs.[98]

This follows the Tri Hita Karana Roadmap for Blended Finance that was introduced by Indonesia in October 2018 during the World Bank–International Monetary Fund Summit in Bali, a roadmap that is supported by Organisation for Economic Co-operation and Development (OECD) partners from governments, development finance institutions, and the private sector. A landmark blended finance model is the Tropical Landscape Finance Facility, which issued a USD95 million sustainability bond with a project preparation and blended finance partnership with UN Environment, the World Agroforestry Centre (which enabled private capital from ADM Capital), and BNP Paribas.[99]

The Philippines

The Philippines has a bank-based economy and has maintained a high level of financial stability since the 1997/98 Asian financial crisis.[100] However, the country's financial depth is modest compared with neighboring emerging economies. The combined market capitalization of listed companies is equivalent to only 84% of the country's gross domestic product (GDP). Meanwhile, the corporate bond market is small (about 34% of the country's GDP in 2019) despite growth in recent years.[101] The Government of the Philippines has implemented several capital market development plans to strengthen the capital markets and enhance their depth (footnote 17).

Recently, the Bangko Sentral ng Pilipinas (BSP), the Bureau of the Treasury, and the Securities and Exchange Commission co-created the Philippines Roadmap on Local Currency Debt Market Development to address the vicious cycle that inhibits the broadening and deepening of the financial sector and to support debt management in the country.[102] The roadmap highlights three immediate priorities: (i) deepening market liquidity, (ii) improving bond pricing and valuation, and (iii) strengthening regulatory oversight and surveillance. Furthermore, the Philippines

[97]   K. Davidson et al. 2019. *Green Infrastructure Investment Opportunities: Indonesia Update Report*. Climate Bonds Initiative. https://www.climatebonds.net/files/reports/giio_indonesia_2019_update_report.pdf.

[98]   K. Kusters. 2018. Landmark $95 million bond for sustainable rubber joint venture in Indonesia. *Landscape News*. 28 February. https://news.globallandscapesforum.org/26318/landmark-95-million-bond-sustainable-rubber-joint-venture-indonesia/.

[99]   Low Carbon Development Indonesia. Low Carbon Development: A Paradigm Shift Towards a Green Economy in Indonesia. https://drive.bappenas.go.id/owncloud/index.php/s/fmSzqdr3Kmv1Ww5#pdfviewer.

[100]   F. G. Dakila Jr. 2020. The development of financial markets in the Philippines and its interaction with monetary policy and financial stability. *BIS Papers No 113*. https://www.bis.org/publ/bppdf/bispap113_p.pdf.

[101]   L. Cao and L. Garcia-Feijoo, eds. 2021. The Emerging Asia-Pacific Capital Markets: Challenges And Opportunities. *CFA Institute Research Foundation Brief*. https://www.cfainstitute.org/-/media/documents/article/rf-brief/rfbr-apac-capital-markets.ashx.

[102]   Government of the Philippines, Bureau of the Treasury. *The Philippine Roadmap: Local Currency Debt Market Development* (Presentation). https://www.treasury.gov.ph/wp-content/uploads/2017/10/Local-Currency-Debt-Market-Development-Roadmap_ppt-1.pdf.

has also taken part in regional partnerships to deepen its local bond market by implementing the ASEAN+3 Multi-Currency Bond Issuance Framework.

While green finance is relatively new in the Philippines, in 2019 the government introduced the Inter-Agency Technical Working Group for Sustainable Finance, which was co-chaired by the Department of Finance and the BSP. The green inter-agency task force seeks to harmonize existing sustainability policies by identifying policy or technical gaps then allocating the appropriate resources to address these gaps. In late 2021, the Philippine Sustainable Finance Guiding Principles were launched as principles-based guidance that helps identify economic activities that contribute to supporting sustainable development, with a focus on addressing the impacts of climate change and encouraging the flow of capital to these activities.[103]

Green Bonds for Long-Term Financing

The Philippines issued the first green bond in the ASEAN region, a USD226 million deal by AP Renewables, in early 2016. AP Renewables also issued the first Climate Bonds-certified green bond, demonstrating market best practice in terms of climate ambition.

As co-chair of the ACMF Sustainable Finance Working Group, the Securities and Exchange Commission of the Philippines leads the country's efforts in green finance. It has played a key role in the creation of the ASEAN Green Bond Standards, ASEAN Social Bond Standards, and ASEAN Sustainable Bond Standards, as well as the ASEAN Sustainable Capital Markets Roadmap.

Banking on Sustainability

The BSP has stated its intention to strengthen its sustainable finance framework to encourage banks to issue more GSS bonds. In 2021, the BSP has a total of USD550 million investment in the BIS Green Bond Fund.[104]

The BSP acknowledges that the impacts of climate change pose a risk to the financial system and will affect the credit and operational risk exposure of banks, which will extend to profitability and solvency if unmitigated.[105] Consequentially, the BSP has considered climate-related weather risk in its inflation forecasting (footnote 105). Further, the BSP has published the Guidelines on Sustainable Finance Framework, requiring the integration of sustainability principles including those addressing environmental and social risks in corporate governance and risk management frameworks, as well as the strategic objectives and operations of banks.[106] Following this, the Environmental and Social Risk Management Framework was released in October 2021, which sets out the expectations on the integration of environmental and social risks in the credit and operational risk management systems of banks.[107]

Green Funds

The Philippines has established a number of funds to facilitate the development of green infrastructure and renewable energy projects. The People's Survival Fund (PSF), a domestic initiative led by the Climate Change Commission (CCC), was established to assist local government units and accredited community organizations

[103] Bangko Sentral ng Pilipinas. *The Philippine Sustainable Finance Guiding Principles*. https://www.bsp.gov.ph/Media_And_Research/Media%20 Releases/2021_10/Sustainable%20Finance%20Guiding%20Principles.pdf.

[104] L. Agcaoili. 2021. BSP invests $550 million in sustainable bonds. *Philstar*. 31 July. https://www.philstar.com/business/2021/07/31/2116411/bsp-invests-550-million-sustainable-bonds.

[105] BIS. 2019. *Benjamin E. Diokno: Sustainable finance towards a climate-resilient Philippine economy* (Speech). https://www.bis.org/review/r191127h.htm.

[106] Bangko Sentral ng Pilipinas, Office of the Governor. Circular No. 1085 Series of 2020-Sustainable Finance Framework. https://www.bsp.gov.ph/ Regulations/Issuances/2020/c1085.pdf.

[107] L. Agcaoili. 2021. Environment, social risk management framework for banks issued by BSP. *Philstar*. 31 October. https://www.philstar.com/ business/2021/10/31/2137876/environment-social-risk-management-framework-banks-issued-bsp.

in implementing climate change adaptation projects that will better equip vulnerable communities to deal with the effects of climate change.[108] Each year, the Government of the Philippines contributes at least PHP1 billion (USD20 million) to the fund, which is funded through the national budget and may be supplemented through contributions from local government units, the private sector, and philanthropic donations. The PSF is targeted at activities—such as water resource management, land management, agriculture, and fisheries—and serves as a guarantee for farmers, agricultural workers, and other stakeholders who require risk insurance.

The Philippines also has access to the Sustainable Energy Programme, which is a joint undertaking of the European Union (EU) and the Philippine Department of Energy. Through this program, the EU has allocated a grant of more than PHP3 billion (USD58 million) to assist the Philippine government to meet its rural electrification targets using renewable energy and to promote energy efficiency.

In addition, the Philippines can access approximately USD89.6 million from the Green Climate Fund to support climate change mitigation and adaptation priorities.[109] Philippine entities accredited by the Green Climate Fund include the Land Bank of the Philippines and the Development Bank of the Philippines.[110]

Viet Nam

The Vietnamese bond market grew to a size of more than USD70 billion in 2021. Over 80% of the volume coming from government debt, with development banks being the second-largest issuer type. In 2017, the Government of Viet Nam issued Decision No.1191/QD-TTg approving the Bond Market Development Roadmap, 2017–2020, with a vision that extends until 2030.[111] The roadmap sets out goals to improve the domestic bond market so that it increases in size to about 45% of GDP by 2020 and 65% of GDP by 2030, and it focuses on measures to improve market depth and liquidity.

Green Bonds for Long-Term Financing

The Viet Nam Green Growth Strategy, 2011–2020 envisaged capital markets playing a key role in achieving the country's climate goals by 2050.[112] This has served as a basis for green finance to grow in Viet Nam. In 2017, the government approved the road map for bond market development, alongside mechanisms and policies for the green bond market, enabling issuers to raise capital for implementing green projects through the issuance of bonds.[113]

In 2020, the government released Decree 153/2020/ND-CP regarding the private placement of corporate bonds and trading of privately placed corporate bonds in the domestic market, and the offering of corporate bonds in the international market.[114] This decree serves as a guideline for the placement and trading of both conventional and green bonds in the onshore and offshore markets. Some notation points under the decree include (i) the definition and overview of corporate green bonds; (ii) principles for issuance of corporate green bonds; (iii) disclosing and reporting regimes for corporate green bonds; and (iv) issuance methods, redemption, and swaps of corporate green bonds.

[108]   Government of the Philippines. People's Survival Fund. https://niccdies.climate.gov.ph/climate-finance/people-survival-fund.

[109]   Green Climate Fund. Philippines. https://www.greenclimate.fund/countries/philippines#documents.

[110]   *BusinessWorld*. 2021. DBP joins UN's Green Climate Fund. 16 July. https://www.bworldonline.com/banking-finance/2021/07/16/383035/dbp-joins-uns-green-climate-fund.

[111]   SaigonRatings. 2018. Decision No. 1191/QD-TTg approving the capital market development roadmap. 10 February. https://phatthinhrating.com/en/decision-no-1191-qd-ttg-approving-the-capital-market-development-roadmap.

[112]   GIZ. 2018. *Viet Nam Green Growth Strategy*. https://www.giz.de/en/ downloads/VietNam-GreenGrowthStrategy-giz2018.pdf.

[113]   Government of Viet Nam. 2017. Decision No. 1191/QD-TTg of the Prime Minister on Approving the bond market development roadmap during 2017–2020, with a vision toward 2030. http://vietnamlawmagazine.vn/decision-no-1191-qd-ttg-of-august-14-2017-6046.html.

[114]   LuatVietnam. 2020. Decree No. 153/2020/ND-CP trading of privately placed corporate bonds in domestic market. https://english.luatvietnam.vn/decree-no-153-2020-nd-cp-dated-december-31-2020-of-the-government-on-provisions-on-private-offering-and-trading-of-corporate-bonds-in-the-domestic-m-196490-Doc1.html.

In 2016, the Ministry of Finance, partnered with the German International Cooperation Agency on a pilot program to issue green bonds in Ho Chi Minh City and Ba Ria Vung Tau province (Table 6).

Table 6: Pilot Green Bond Issuance Programs in Viet Nam

Project 1: Ho Chi Minh City

- Type of bonds: green municipal bonds
- Term of bonds: 15 years
- Total volume: VND523.5 billion (approximately USD23 million)
- Purposes: funding 11 projects related to sustainable water management, adaptation to climate change, and infrastructure

Project 2: Ba Ria Vung Tau Province

- Type of bonds: green municipal bonds
- Term of bonds: 5 years
- Total volume: VND80 billion (approximately USD4 million)
- Purposes: funding a project related to sustainable water management

Source: Ministry of Finance. 2017. *Prospect of the Green Bond Market in Viet Nam.* http://gizmacro.ciem.org.vn/Content/files/3-Presentation%20and%20Reports/Green%20Financial%20Sector%20Reform /TL%20Hoi%20nghi%20phat%20trien%20thi%20 truong%20von%20xanh%20EN.pdf.

Due to the lack of an appropriate legal framework to support issuance, no corporate green bond issuances have taken place in Viet Nam to date. With the introduction of Decree No. 153, and the ongoing development of the Vietnamese financial markets, corporate green bonds are expected to be issued in the near future.

Green Index

The Ministry of Finance issued Circular No. 155 on Disclosure of Information on the Securities Market in 2015 to assist businesses in disclosing information about green finance activities.[115] The Green and Sustainable Index, which tracks the performance of the top 20 sustainable stocks in the VN100 (the top 100 listed companies on the Ho Chi Minh Stock Exchange), was piloted from January to July 2017 and launched on the Ho Chi Minh Stock Exchange in July 2017.[116]

Banks and Green Credits

Viet Nam is a bank-based economy, with the banking system financing approximately 70% of the economy's capital needs.[117] As a result, the local banking system is a critical component of the country's green financial market development. Indeed, the State Bank of Vietnam has been a vocal supporter of green economy campaigns. The State Bank of Vietnam issued Directive No. 03/CT-NHNN in 2015 to encourage green credit growth and to manage environmental and social risks in credit-granting activities.[118] Table 7 provides some examples of green credit programs in Viet Nam.

---

[115]   Government of Vietnam. 2015. Circular 155/2015-TT-BTC on Disclosure of Information on the Securities Market." https://cms.luatvietnam.vn/Download.aspx?file=2015/15228793.pdf.

[116]   https://sseinitiative.org/stock-exchange/hsx/.

[117]   International Monetary Fund. 2017. *Viet Nam (selected issues).* https://www.elibrary.imf.org/view/journals/002/2017/191/002.2017.issue-191-en.xml.

[118]   State Bank of Vietnam. 2015. Directive on Promoting Green Credit Growth and Environmental – Social Risks Management in Credit Granting Activities. 24 March. https://vanbanphapluat.co/directive-no-03-ct-nhnn-2015-green-credit-growth-environmental-social-risks-credit-granting.

Table 7: Green Credit Programs in Viet Nam

Proponents	Amount	Intended Customers	Participants	Results
SBV[a]	Approximately USD100 million	SMEs with green projects	Vietcombank, BIDV, Agribank, and Sacombank	• To date, 26 projects in the program on renewable energy, waste management, and organic agriculture have been financed. • The interest rates applicable to SMEs is 1–3 percentage points lower than market interest rates. • Banks participating in the program are refinanced from SBV at interest rates 1 percentage point lower than usual.
Agribank and Viet Nam Development Bank[b]	60% of the required capital for the project (about USD18 million)	Solar Power Plant TTC Phong Dien in Hue province	Agribank and Viet Nam Development Bank	• Construction for the solar power project was started in the fourth quarter of 2017 and finished after 1 year. • Agribank Thua Thien-Hue and Agribank Gia Lai branches will finance 30% of the total investment, while VDB Thua Thien-Hue and VDB Quang Tri will cover the rest.
Vietcombank and Japan International Cooperation Bank[c]	USD200 million	Solar and wind power projects in Viet Nam	Vietcombank and Japan Bank for International Cooperation	Not informed yet (the cooperation agreement between VCB and JBIC was signed in May 2019).
Agribank and Central Power Corporation[d]	VND735 billion	Central power solar project in Khanh Hoa province	Agribank	The power plant was completed and put into operation in May 2019.
TPBank and the Global Climate Partnership Fund[e]	USD20 million	Green projects in Viet Nam	TPBank and the Global Climate Partnership Fund (GCPF)	Not informed yet (the cooperation agreement between VCB and JBIC was signed in May 2019).

JBIC = Japan Bank for International Cooperation, SBV = State Bank of Vietnam, SME = small and medium-sized enterprise, USD = United States dollar, VCB = Vietcombank, VND = Vietnamese dong.

[a] GIZ. 2016. Green Financial Sector Reform in Viet Nam. http://gizmacro.ciem.org.vn/Content/files/2-Communication%20 Materials/Green%20Financial%20Sector%20Reform%20in%20Vietnam.pdf.

[b] Nhan Dan. 2017. Banks Provide funding for Phong Dien Solar Power Plant Construction. https://en.nhandan.org.vn/business/ investment/item/5482202-banks-provide-funding-for-phong-dien-solar-power-plant-construction.html.

[c] Vietcombank. 2019. JBIC Loans 200 Million USD to Vietcombank to Support Renewable Energy Projects in Viet Nam. https://portal.vietcombank.com.vn/en-Us/News/newsevent/Pages/Vietcombank.aspx?ItemID=5873.

[d] EVN. 2018. EVNCPC Borrows VND 735 Billion from Agribank to Construct Central Power Corporation's Solar Power Plant. https://en.evn.com.vn/d6/news/EVNCPC-borrows-VND-735-billion-from-Agribank-to-construct-Central-Power-Corporations-Solar-Power-Plant-66-163-1317.aspx.

[e] See https://tpb.vn/tin-tuc/tin-tpbank/tpbank-va-gcpf-ky-ket-hop-dong-cho-vay-tin-dung-xanh-20-trieu-usd.

Source: Authors' compilation.

At the end of 2020, the National Assembly of Viet Nam passed the new Environmental Protection Law, 2020 with major changes compared to the previous version.[119] Among the changes are the inclusion of the definition, general requirements of green bonds, and potential incentives applicable to eligible issuers, which will be specified in the sub-law documents. A green taxonomy is being developed together with the promulgation of the law. This new law is expected to be introduced in 2022.

Brunei Darussalam

Brunei Darussalam is diversifying its economy by developing new industries to gradually reduce its reliance on the oil and gas sector. The government has outlined its development objectives for the next several decades in a policy document titled *Wawasan Brunei 2035* (*Brunei Vision 2035*). By 2035, the policy document envisions the financial sector in Brunei Darussalam playing a critical role in transforming the domestic economy by providing financial intermediation for overall economic development and contributing at least 8% of national GDP. The government's economic reform program, which aims to diversify and grow Brunei Darussalam's economy, will create new opportunities for banks, insurance companies, and the capital market.[120]

To this end, the Brunei Darussalam Central Bank (BDCB) developed the *Brunei Darussalam Financial Sector Blueprint, 2016–2025* to outline the ways in which Brunei Darussalam will strengthen and expand existing relationships with international investors, financial institutions, and financial centers, particularly in the provision of Islamic financial services. The blueprint emphasizes the growing opportunity to promote investing based on sustainable, responsible, and impact criteria, including ESG criteria, in order to generate long-term financial returns and positive societal impact as part of fund-management business development strategies.[121]

In 2020, the Ministry of Finance and Economy, issued the economic blueprint for Brunei Darussalam, *Towards a Dynamic and Sustainable Economy*. The blueprint includes six aspirations toward preservation of a sustainable environment while maintaining growth through the following strategic priorities:

(i)   Promote the sustainability of the environment by ensuring natural assets and resources are well-preserved.

(ii)   Promote economic growth through green growth initiatives and a sustainable blue economy.

(iii) Invest in and promote sustainable businesses and technology to both increase productivity and conserve the environment.[122]

Cambodia

The Securities and Exchange Regulator of Cambodia (SERC) was inaugurated in 2008 as an autonomous government agency and the sole regulator of the securities sector in Cambodia, including infrastructure providers, market participants, and intermediaries for participant activities in the securities market. Meanwhile, the National Bank of Cambodia, established in 1954, is responsible for setting and executing monetary policy and conducting related activities. The National Bank of Cambodia also regulates and supervises banks and financial institutions, including in the interbank market, and oversees the country's payment systems.

---

[119] L. M. Thuy. New law on environment protection in Vietnam. https://static1.squarespace.com/static/50c0b136e4b01ad287768e06/t/60dae527cf 27143cc9bb24a6/1624958249043/2021+6+15+New+environment+protection+law+blog+%28EN%29+1.1.pdf.

[120] ADB. 2017. *ASEAN+3 Bond Market Guide 2017 Brunei Darussalam*. Manila. https://www.adb.org/sites/default/files/publication/371561/asean3-bond-market-bru-2017.pdf.

[121] Autoriti Monetari Brunei Darussalam. 2016. *Brunei Darussalam Financial Sector Blueprint (2016-2025)*. https://bab.org.bn/wp-content/uploads/2019/06/AMBD-BRUNEI-DARUSSALAM-FINANCIAL-SECTOR-BLUEPRINT-2016-2025-FINAL_compressed.pdf.

[122] Government of Brunei Darussalam, Ministry of Finance and Economy. 2020. Towards a Dynamic and Sustainable Economy Economic Blueprint for Brunei Darussalam. https://www.mofe.gov.bn/Shared%20Documents/OTHERS/banner/Brunei%20Darussalam%27s%20Economic%20 Blueprint.pdf.

Hattha Bank Plc.'s bond issuance in 2018 marked the first-ever corporate bond in Cambodia. By 2020, three commercial banks, two microfinance institutions, and one import–export company had listed in the bond market,[123] with the equivalent of USD70 million of these bonds guaranteed by the Credit Guarantee and Investment Facility (CGIF).[124] However, GSS bonds have yet to be issued in the capital market.

The SERC recently approved the ASEAN Green Bond Standards, which provide guidance to investors and issuers on investing with an ESG mandate in mind. In addition, SERC licensed new financial products such as private equity, real estate investment trusts, mutual funds, and other types of fund management firms. Both issuers and investors benefit from tax incentives. Regular government bonds are expected to begin trading in the near future and will serve as a benchmark for the pricing of all financial instruments.[125] Several financial institutions have received credit ratings from both international and domestic credit rating agencies, and institutional investors such as life insurance companies have expressed interest in corporate bond investors as a means of diversifying their portfolios.

Developing the energy sector infrastructure is a priority for Cambodia's national economic development toward sustainability, as the country is heavily reliant on imported fossil fuels and electricity, resulting in some of the highest domestic electricity prices in ASEAN. Green bonds and loans could be used to finance energy companies that wish to develop local renewable energy sources.

Lao People's Democratic Republic

The Lao Securities Exchange was officially established in October 2010 under the authority of the Lao Securities Commission. The first transaction occurred 3 months later in January 2011. The Government of the Lao People's Democratic Republic (PDR) and the Lao Securities Exchange-listed EDL Generation Public Company (EDL-Gen), an electricity energy firm in the Lao PDR operating 10 wholly owned hydropower plants, 1 solar plant, and 5 independent power plants, have issued 14 sovereign bonds. Three of the 14 bonds are USD-denominated with a combined volume of USD312 million, while the other 11 are THB-denominated and have a total size of THB22.5 billion (USD750 million). The decision to issue THB-denominated government debt reflects the lack of investment in the region and leverages the relatively well-developed Thai capital market to support infrastructure projects.[126] A green sovereign would naturally increase the profile of the Lao PDR and its commitments to sustainable development, and there is proven demand in neighboring capital markets including Thailand, Malaysia, and Singapore.

Hydropower dominates the energy sector. EDL-Gen is accustomed to using the debt markets and has issued vanilla bonds in both USD and THB. If there were sufficient green assets on the balance sheet, EDL-Gen could consider issuing under the green label in other ASEAN capital markets to extend the investor base and raise the profile of the Lao PDR in the green finance space.[127]

---

[123] National Bank of Cambodia. Financial Stability Review 2020. https://www.nbc.org.kh/download_files/publication/fsr_eng/Final_FSR_2020_English.pdf.

[124] Credit Guarantee & Investment Facility. Guarantee Portfolio. https://www.cgif-abmi.org/guarantee-portfolio.

[125] G. T. Eu. 2021. Cambodia law allowing government bond issuance takes effect, report says. *Asia Asset Management*. 5 January. https://www.asiaasset.com/post/24163-cambodiacsx-gte-0104.

[126] Climate Bonds Initiative. 2020. *ASEAN State of the Green Finance Market 2019*. https://www.climatebonds.net/system/tdf/reports/cbi_asean_sotm_2019_final.pdf?file=1&type=node&id=47010&force=0.

[127] Southeast Asian Journal of Economics. 2020. *Securities Commission Organization and Stock Exchange Development in Viet Nam and Laos*. 8 (2). https://www.researchgate.net/publication/341398464_Securities_Commission_Organization_and_Stock_Exchange_Development_in_Viet_Nam_and_Laos.

Lessons Learned from Other Markets

Certain barriers are common to many global GSS markets. In certain instances, the ASEAN+3 region can *apply what has been learned from other regions. However, there are* notable differences between the ASEAN+3 member economies and the countries listed in this section such as differing degrees of sophistication and market depth. Nonetheless, developments in these markets and regions may provide important lessons for the ASEAN+3 region.

Brazil

Despite a difficult macroeconomic outlook as a result of the economic downturn between 2014 and 2016, as well as the COVID-19 outbreak, green finance in Brazil has enormous growth potential and could help the country meet its climate goals. Since 2012, the Brazilian government and other key actors have developed a number of significant green finance initiatives.

The Brazil Green Finance Initiative has helped to expand the institutional investor base and connected players from industry and finance.

The Brazil Green Finance Initiative, a collaboration between the Business Council for Sustainable Development of Brazil in partnership with Climate Bonds, was developed to bring together high-level representatives from Brazil's pension funds, public and private banks, insurance companies, local market institutions, and key industrial sectors to promote policy and market mechanisms for robust sustainable investments in Brazil.[128] Climate Bonds and the Brazil Green Finance Initiative helped investors representing BRL1.8 trillion in assets sign a joint Green Bonds Statement in 2017 to show their support for green bonds. The assets under management of the Brazil Green Finance Initiative total around USD1 trillion.

Two green funds were established (one by BNDES in 2017 and the other by BrasilPrev in 2019) to refinance renewable energy portfolios as part of this initiative. In addition, Brazil's Securities and Exchange Commission and the Brazilian Development Association, in collaboration with the Inter-American Development Bank, launched the Financial Innovation Laboratory. One of its cross-sector working groups is tasked with researching, developing, and piloting financial instruments to boost climate-related investment.[129]

Private companies can obtain upfront financing for green investments.

Debt capital markets can be used by private companies and companies operating under government concessions to obtain upfront financing for green investments. As a result, these businesses could issue green bonds to raise the funds needed to build the necessary infrastructure on a local level. Corporate bonds accounted for 75.3 % of Brazil's green bond market (USD7.5 billion) and 66.3 % of Brazil's LCY green bond market (BRL2.65).

Infrastructure debentures are one of Brazil's most popular financing instruments. They can generally offer lower funding costs, longer maturities, better guarantee requirements, and more appealing returns to investors than traditional bank lending.

Since 2011, a new type of infrastructure debenture, incentivized debentures, has grown in popularity in the Brazilian market. Incentivized infrastructure debentures, which are governed by Law 12.431, exempt individual investors

[128] Climate Bonds Initiative. Brazil Green Finance Initiative. https://www.climatebonds.net/market/country/brazil/green-finance-initiative.
[129] K. Davidson et al. 2020. Green Infrastructure Investment Opportunities - Brazil 2019. *Technical note*. Inter-American Development Bank. https://publications.iadb.org/publications/english/document/Green-Infrastructure-Investment-Opportunities-Brazil-2019.pdf.

from paying income tax, and as a result, this product is almost entirely absorbed by retail investors as an appealing form of personal investment.

Decree 10.387/20, issued in June 2020, established a fast track for infrastructure debentures with social and environmental benefits (under Law 12.431/11). The new regulation, proposed by Brazil's Ministry of Economy and developed with assistance from the Inter-American Development Bank's Financial Innovation Lab, encourages more green projects to fill the country's infrastructure gaps.[130]

B3 has played a critical role in ramping up responsible investments in Brazil.

As more companies embrace stakeholder capitalism and investors express greater interest in socially responsible investing, ESG has moved into the mainstream.[131] B3, the largest Brazilian stock exchange, supported sustainable finance flows by pioneering the dissemination and promotion of the ESG agenda as early as 2005 by devising the world's fourth sustainability index, the Corporate Sustainability Index.[132] This helped bring the concept of sustainability to the Brazilian market such that in 2012, B3 recommended listed companies to provide ESG reporting (footnote 131) or, if not, to explain why through the "report or explain" initiative before publishing two Sustainability Guides, with the most recent edition published in 2016.[133] Since then, it has developed several additional ESG indices tracking companies' corporate governance, climate change practices, and general ESG aspects (footnote 131).

Nordic Countries

The "Nordic Model" is key to understanding ASEAN+3's financing needs.

In terms of financial management, the Nordic countries have taken a unique approach. The Nordic Model, as it has developed in Denmark, Finland, and Sweden, is based on decentralization and collaboration between regions and municipalities to provide a wide range of services to the people they serve.[134] Local and regional governments bear a significant fiscal responsibility, including taxing power and the ability to borrow money.

This puts a lot of assets and financing decisions in the hands of municipalities. Indeed, local governments have significant fiscal autonomy and the ability to issue bonds to fund the delivery of public services and to improve the asset base they manage. Bond programs are becoming more popular, albeit primarily on a domestic level, as funding requirements at the city or even municipal level can be minimal or infrequent.

Local government funding agencies play a pivotal role in the local debt market.

As a pooled funding model for the public sector, local government funding agencies (LGFAs) are common in the region. They are well-established institutions with a specific mandate to fund municipalities, cities, counties, regions, government-backed businesses, and government-backed agencies.

---

[130] See https://www.gov.br/casacivil/pt-br/assuntos/noticias/2020/junho/debentures-verdes-governo-federal-publica-decreto-que-incentiva-projetos-de-infraestrutura-ambientalmente-sustentaveis.

[131] Nasdaq. 2021. Era of Impact: How B3 Pioneered ESG in the Brazilian Market. 27 August. https://www.nasdaq.com/articles/era-of-impact%3A-how-b3-pioneered-esg-in-the-brazilian-market-2021-08-27.

[132] B3. Corporate Sustainability Index (ISE B3). https://www.b3.com.br/en_us/market-data-and-indices/indices/sustainability-indices/corporate-sustainability-index-ise.htm.

[133] GIZ. 2020. Mainstreaming Sustainability in Brazil's Financial Sector. http://www.labinovacaofinanceira.com/wp-content/uploads/2020/12/GIZ-Mainstreaming-sustainability-ENG-final.pdf.

[134] KommuneKredit, Kommuninvest, MuniFin. 2021. *The Nordic Model: Local Government, Global Competitiveness in Denmark, Sweden, and Finland.*

Except for KBN, which is owned by the state, LGFAs are owned by member municipalities. Although municipalities are not required to join, the majority have done so. The ownership structure is similar to that of credit unions, with the owners and borrowers being the same entity.

LGFAs have a significant advantage in terms of aggregation. LGFAs can raise large sums of money, including through benchmark bond deals, and use the proceeds to lend to even the smallest of government entities. LGFAs' sovereign credit ratings and larger deal sizes enable them to obtain competitive bond pricing, which they pass on to their member municipalities in the form of low loan interest rates.

Although some public sector entities have begun to tap bond markets directly, LGFAs remain the most viable funding source for smaller cities, municipalities, and municipality- and state-owned businesses.

Common Issues and Existing Impediments in ASEAN+3

The ASEAN+3 market is not homogeneous. The extent to which particular barriers affect sustainable finance in each economy varies depending on the degree of development. Some of the key barriers are discussed below.

Lack of market awareness and capacity. A critical impediment for all emerging markets is a lack of awareness and understanding of GSS bonds on a local level. This will inevitably change and grow as transactions increase, but it presents a "chicken-and-egg" situation in the early stages. Potential advisers and service providers are hesitant to invest in the capacity necessary to verify, structure, and advise on GSS bonds, and issuers have limited access to low-cost local service providers who can provide GSS bond advice. Due to a lack of market awareness, new deals may be unable to enter the market.

(i)   **Issuers.** Among bond issuers, market education on the existence, benefits, and purpose of GSS bonds can increase market players' knowledge of the GSS bond issuance opportunity. Likewise, awareness can also be increased through large benchmark-sized issues from supranational and other issuers with sufficiently high credit ratings.

(ii)   **Investors.** While the investor base is substantial, awareness of ESG issues remains low. GSS bonds are an excellent entry point for investors with limited experience in ESG investing because their structure is straightforward and they behave similarly to vanilla bonds. As is the case in the majority of countries, there are currently no ESG investment requirements.

Lack of market guidance and standards. The lack of market guidance and standards can make it difficult for the local market to determine which assets or projects qualify as GSS. The Climate Bonds Standard, for example, is a globally accepted standard that can help in this regard. External reviewer reports can also reassure investors that the bond they are investing in is aligned with the Green Bond Principles (GBP), Social Bond Principles (SBP), and Sustainability Bond Guidelines (SBG), and meets the Climate Bonds Standard.

Lack of standardized guidelines. While the proliferation of regional and national sustainable finance guidelines has been beneficial in kickstarting the local market, the absence of global market practices can be confusing for investors and act as a barrier to the overall market—particularly when it comes to facilitating cross-border capital flows.[135] Currently, the GSS bond and green *sukuk* markets in most jurisdictions operate under a voluntary framework that establishes best practices for investors. Green *sukuk* can use a variety of GSS bond frameworks, as

---

[135]   The Sustainabilist. 2018. Developing the Green Sukuk Market. 23 June. https://thesustainabilist.ae/developing-the-green-sukuk-market.

well as green-*sukuk*-specific frameworks and standards. Investors have far too few tools to ensure that their money is making a difference. Investors, potential issuers, and policymakers can more easily identify eligible assets and attract investment by using common definitions of GSS bonds across global markets.[136]

Slightly higher transaction costs. When compared to conventional bonds and loan financing, the costs of issuing sustainable bonds are relatively higher. Some costs are universal (e.g., obtaining a credit rating, drafting a bond prospectus, and calculating legal fees), while others are unique to GSS bonds (e.g., obtaining a second-party opinion or certification). A GSS bond issuer is responsible for the additional costs and expenses of an independent third-party review of proceeds. For large transactions, these costs are insignificant, but they can be a deterrent for smaller transactions.

Impact reporting requirements. The *Post-Issuance Report* published by Climate Bonds confirms that some stakeholders have cited impact reporting commitments as a major roadblock to more GSS bond issuance. The perceptions of difficulty and cost are related to an initially steep learning curve, which should flatten over time as issuers gain reporting experience.

Limited number of bankable GSS projects. To raise capital via the issuance of a green bond, the issuer must have bankable projects that enable investors to make investment decisions based on their risk tolerance and the underlying projects' risk-return profiles. However, a wide variety of green projects—including those involving water, pollution control, land use, natural resource management, and climate change adaptation—are deemed unbankable due to their low profitability and cash flows, as well as their lack of track record. Inadequate bankability of green projects obstructs project developers (i.e., potential green bond issuers) from raising capital for their projects, including through the issuance of green bonds.

Social projects are often viewed as unbankable. Investors and issuers frequently believe that social bonds are generally issued by governments and/or multilateral development banks to finance and/or refinance projects that contribute to positive social outcomes, but that they do not provide investors with sufficient financial returns to compensate them for their investments. Furthermore, social projects do not necessitate large capital investments. As a result, corporate issuers are frequently overlooking or unconcerned about how their operations can address social issues. One example is that social bond issuers can prioritize local job creation and allow workers to stay close to their families. These bonds can be created via securitization, where single instrument can create large deal sizes that meet investor needs while financing multiple individual businesses, including SMEs.

As the market grows, these barriers are also reduced. For example, as the number of green *sukuk* has grown, so has investor awareness and comfort with these new products. Furthermore, as these transactions become more common, the issuance process becomes less complicated, while the cost of external review may decrease as issuers use local talent rather than bringing in international experts.

---

[136]   Climate Bonds Initiative. 2019. *Brazil Green Infrastructure Investment Opportunities.* https://www.climatebonds.net/files/reports/cbi_giio_2019_02c_0.pdf.

4 Green Investment Opportunities in ASEAN+3 Economies

Across ASEAN+3, central and local governments aim to mobilize billions of dollars of capital for new public works projects. While there is a large variety of existing green infrastructure projects and assets in the region, there is a crucial need across all economies for further investment in projects that not only contribute to the long-term development of communities but also help achieve the green transition required for economies to achieve their environmental goals. In particular, there is a need for such green investment to be conducted in local ASEAN+3 currencies to foster more sustainable debt markets, minimize long-term risks of hard currency issuance, and engage existing local investors and capital markets.

Several economy-specific analyses have been undertaken to understand the market context and determine priority actions. This recommendation uses the well-recognized Climate Bonds Taxonomy and Sector Criteria to determine which projects and assets can be considered green. However, there are many other standards and schemes available to measure and define a project's "greenness" and eligibility, including various national, bilateral, and global standards, as well as the principles introduced in *the ASEAN Taxonomy for Sustainable Finance (Version 1)*.

Methodology

The following section explores LCY green infrastructure investment opportunities and case studies among members of ASEAN+3 in four key sectors: (i) renewable energy, (ii) low-carbon transport, (iii) sustainable water management, and (iv) sustainable waste management. Although not included in these segments, the region is also host to green projects in other sectors like green buildings, sustainable agriculture and forestry, and tourism.

Accordingly, metrics were used to classify the green infrastructure investment opportunities by status:

(i)   completed projects: high profile, recently completed projects;

(ii)   projects under construction: major projects that are under construction; and

(iii) planned projects: major projects that have not yet begun construction but have been announced and/or have undergone business case planning and/or have been allocated budget.

Climate Bonds Taxonomy and the Climate Bonds Standard and Certification Scheme

There are eight climate-related sectors in the Climate Bonds Taxonomy.[137] The taxonomy's goal is to promote common broad "green" definitions across global markets in order to foster the development of a unified green bond market. A labeling scheme for bonds and other debt instruments is provided by the Climate Bonds Standard and Certification Scheme.

The sector criteria for the Climate Bonds Standard and Certification Scheme establishes eligibility criteria or thresholds that must be met for assets to be on track for a zero-carbon future by 2050. Technical expert groups, with input from industry representatives, developed the criteria based on climate science.

---

[137]   Climate Bonds Initiative. 2020. CBI Database. https://www.climatebonds.net/standard/taxonomy.

Renewable Energy

Across ASEAN+3, renewable energy generation, distribution, and transmission assets are owned privately, by state-owned enterprises, or by local government entities. State-owned electricity companies generally account for the majority of energy output, but this varies from economy to economy.

Renewable energy project developers and asset owners should have access to a variety of funding options to maximize and accelerate the transition to clean energy such as from banks, specialized project financiers, debt clubs, investment funds, direct investors, and capital markets.

Green bonds are ideally suited to large renewable energy projects or asset portfolios and can be structured in several ways depending on the issuer and investor needs. This includes project bonds, corporate bonds, covered bonds, asset-backed securities (ABS), and Shari'ah-compliant *sukuk* issuance. The aggregation of smaller projects can be done through securitization or by banks providing green loans and refinancing in the green bond and *sukuk* market. Renewable energy funds are also being used to support greenfield projects and stimulate innovation. Renewable energy project financing currently consists of 31.8% of green bond financing in the ASEAN+3 region, totaling approximately USD83.5 billion across regional markets and 20.3% of LCY green bond financing (USD34.4 billion).

The 20-year green *sukuk* issued by Pasukhas Group Bhd. for MYR17 million (USD3.9 million) out of a facility size of MYR200 million) with proceeds allocated to a hydropower plant is one example of an LCY bond being used to finance renewable energy projects in ASEAN+3. Danajamin Nasional, a financial guarantor co-owned by Bank Negara Malaysia and the Ministry of Finance, has guaranteed the *sukuk*. Rizal Commercial Banking Corporation provided a second opinion as well as a green rating.

In April 2018, UiTM Solar Power Sdn. Bhd. issued a green SRI *sukuk* worth MYR222 million (USD55.9 million) to fund the construction of a 50-megawatt (MW) solar power plant in Gambang, Pahang, Malaysia. It was the world's first university to issue a green *sukuk*.

Low-Carbon Transport

Transportation infrastructure is traditionally funded by government budgets throughout ASEAN+3, but there are a variety of funding structures available to encourage private sector participation in the long-term financing required for transportation projects. Green bonds, outright asset purchases, public–private partnerships (PPPs), and the securitization of green assets are all examples of this.

Concessional loans backed by the government are a new structure in ASEAN+3 that give governments more leverage against public transportation revenue streams.

The use of LCY sustainable bonds for financing transport is already prevalent in the PRC; Hong Kong, China; Japan; and Thailand. But it is relatively nascent elsewhere totaling 25.4% of total green bond issuance and 25.6% of LCY green bond issuance (USD66.9 billion and USD43.6 billion, respectively). In 2017, China Development Bank issued a CNY5 billion (USD766.87 million) Guangdong–Hong Kong–Macao Greater Bay Area Clean Transportation Construction-themed green bond. The Industrial and Commercial Bank of China issued a USD3.2 billion Guangdong–Hong Kong–Macao Greater Bay Area-themed green bond with proceeds allocated for low-emission transportation in 2019. Hong Kong, China's MTR; Guangzhou Metro Group; Shenzhen Metro Group; and Japan's JRTT have also issued several LCY green bonds for railway and transport construction. In 2019, Rizal Commercial Banking Corporation issued a PHP15.0 billion green bond with the UOP allocated for low-carbon transportation (along with energy, buildings, and waste).

Sustainable Water Management

The vast majority of water and water-related infrastructure continues to be publicly owned or funded by multilateral banks and bilateral government agencies. Sovereign and sub-sovereign green bonds can and have been used to complement the funding of public water infrastructure issued by local governments and utility companies such as in Viet Nam and Hong Kong, China.

Currently, sustainable water management comprises 10.1% of the total green bond volume issued in ASEAN+3, totaling some USD26.5 billion worth of financing, and 9.5% of LCY green bond volume (USD16.1 billion). One of the first major green bonds issued for sustainable water management came from Beijing Enterprises Water Group, which issued CNY2.8 billion twice in 2016 for a variety of water supply, recycling, and flood adaptation and management projects.

One green *sukuk* has been issued in Malaysia where the UOP is allocated for water infrastructure. Pasukhas Group (a nonfinancial corporate) issued a MYR200 million green bond in February 2019 with the UOP allocated for energy, buildings, water, waste, and land use. In 2018, Viet Nam's People's Committee of Ba Ria Vung Tau Province issued a green bond worth VND80 billion (USD4 million) for the financing of water resources management, and in 2020 Japan's Kanagawa Prefecture issued a JPY5 billion (USD48 million) green bond for flood disaster protection strategies.

Sustainable Waste Management

The majority of ASEAN+3's major waste management assets and projects are publicly owned, with public funding primarily going toward waste treatment facilities and waste-to-energy infrastructure. Typically, waste treatment facilities require a sizable capital investment. Municipalities may be able to fund projects through PPPs or the issuance of green bonds.

Some notable examples of LCY bonds for sustainable waste management include Thai utility company Global Power Synergy Corporation's THB5.0 billion (USD160 million) of green bonds in August 2020 for waste sorting, recycling, and waste-to-energy projects. Funds have been used to finance the construction of a waste-to-energy and refuse-derived fuel plant in Rayong, Thailand for the Provincial Electricity Authority, generating 9.8 MW of capacity. Singapore's National Environment Agency's 2021 SGD1.65 billion (USD1.23 billion) green bond's UOP is exclusively dedicated to sustainable waste management systems—with the first eligible project being its Tuas Nexus Integrated Waste Management facility—including systems for incinerable and food waste, household recyclables, dewatered sludge, and wastewater processing.

Green Buildings

Globally, the buildings and construction sector has been a large contributor to carbon dioxide emissions, having contributed around 39% of total carbon dioxide emissions in 2018.[138] Thus, embracing low-carbon approaches for buildings is essential for developing low-carbon economies in the ASEAN+3 region. Several green building rating tools have been developed in the region, including Malaysia's Green Building Index (GBI); the PRC's Green

---

[138]   World Green Building Council. 2019 Global Status Report for Buildings and Construction. https://www.worldgbc.org/news-media/2019-global-status-report-buildings-and-construction.

Building Evaluation Standard; Hong Kong, China's Building Environmental Assessment Method (BEAM) Plus; the Philippines' Green Building Code (GBC) and Building for Ecologically Responsive Design Excellence (BERDE); and international certification schemes like Leadership in Energy and Environmental Design (LEED) certification.

Low-carbon buildings currently account for just 20.1% of green bond issuances in ASEAN+3 (USD52.9 billion) and a similar 20.3% of LCY issuance in ASEAN+3 (USD34.5 billion). One notable example comes from PNB Merdeka Ventures Sdn. Bhd.'s MYR690 million green *sukuk* (USD170 million) used to finance its Merdeka PNB 118 Tower, the tallest building in Malaysia, with the goal of being triple-platinum ratings using the international LEED, Malaysia's GBI, and another Malaysian standard, GreenRE.[139] In the Philippines, Arthaland Corp. issued a PHP3.0 billion (USD59 million) ASEAN green bond in 2020 to finance its portfolio, which is required to achieve multiple green building standards, including international standards such as LEED and the International Finance Corporation's Excellence in Design for Greater Efficiencies, as well as the local BERDE rating program.

139   Neapoli. Merdeka PNB 118. https://www.neapoli.com/portfolio/neapoli-2.

5 | Recommendations

This report separates the recommendations between three distinct areas: supply side, demand side, and the market ecosystem.

Supply Side

Sovereign GSS Bond Issuances

A sovereign GSS bond can be a lynchpin for market development. Globally, 2021 saw a significant increase in sovereign issuance, with six debut green or sustainable bonds and three returns-to-market occurring in Q3 alone. Outside of ASEAN+3, two significant green sovereign labeled bonds were issued:

(i) In September 2021, the Government of the UK, host of COP26 in Glasgow, issued an AA-rated, GBP10.0 billion (USD13.6 billion) green gilt on the back of a 10 times oversubscribed order book. This was followed a month later by a second green gilt worth GBP6 billion, with a substantial retail offering included and was 12 times oversubscribed.[140]

(ii) In October 2021, the European Commission issued an AAA-rated EUR12.0 billion green bond (USD14.0 billion) that was 11 times oversubscribed, the first issuance of what has been telegraphed as a EUR225.0 billion green program.[141]

Emerging market sovereign issuance has the potential to direct green capital flows to areas most in need. Multiple emerging market countries have issued thematic bonds that have helped to grow the countries' profile in the GSS space. In Indonesia, the major driver of market development has been sovereign and government-backed entities' issuance.[142]

In 2020, the Government of Thailand, via its Public Debt Management Office (PDMO), led the way through a first-time sovereign sustainability bond—the first of a kind issuance by a sovereign in ASEAN (footnote 142). Singapore raised SGD1.7 billion for its first green bond in September 2021, and Malaysia sold the first Sustainability *Sukuk* worth USD800 million in April 2021. These issuances not only generated capital for the government's environmental and social projects, but they also generated confidence in LCY sustainable debt markets, further earmarking finance for GSS assets and projects.

---

[140] Government of the United Kingdom. 2021. Second UK Green Gilt raises further £6 billion for green projects. News release. 21 October. https://www.gov.uk/government/news/second-uk-green-gilt-raises-further-6-billion-for-green-projects.

[141] European Commission. 2021. NextGenerationEU: European Commission successfully issues first green bond to finance the sustainable recovery. News release. 12 October. https://ec.europa.eu/commission/presscorner/detail/en/IP_21_5207.

[142] Climate Bonds Initiative. ASEAN Sustainable Finance State of the Market 2020. https://www.climatebonds.net/resources/reports/asean-sustainable-finance-state-market-2020.

GSS bonds offer governments an opportunity to rethink their spending. Sovereign social and sustainability bonds have demonstrated that they enable issuers to grow and diversify their investor base; they also achieve significant price benefits in liquid and other currencies. Additionally, issuance energizes internal government discussions about growing green assets and pursuing projects that allow for repeated issuance. Due to consistent premium pricing in secondary markets, several sovereign GSS bond issuers benefited from tighter pricing in 2021, including Germany; France; Indonesia; the UK; the EU; and Hong Kong, China.[143] This lower cost of capital is critical in the ASEAN+3 region, where lending costs are frequently significantly higher than in developed markets.

Sovereign issuance enhances clarity on policy gaps. Prior to issuing sovereign GSS bonds, governments must consider green and/or sustainable projects and activities in their economic development plan. This will then trigger identifying funding sources. The development of a sovereign green bond framework involves a budget check (green-tagging) to determine which expenditures qualify for inclusion in the green bond. This procedure has the potential to reveal inconsistencies in government policy and information. For instance, Chile's green bond development uncovered a need for greater transparency in government spending and resulted in the revision of building codes. Sovereigns can follow France's lead, which assigns a green coefficient to each budget line based on its greenness in relation to the EU Taxonomy's six environmental priorities: climate change mitigation, climate change adaptation, water management, circular economy, pollution, and biodiversity.[144]

Sovereign GSS bonds can catalyze local sustainable bond markets. Sovereign bonds provide benchmark pricing, liquidity, and a demonstration effect for domestic issuers, thereby assisting in the growth of a local market in a manner consistent with domestic sustainable capital market initiatives. Additionally, they increase investor appetite, creating opportunities for other issuers. With the International Energy Agency's *World Energy Outlook 2021* estimating that emerging and developing economies will need to spend 70% of the additional USD4 trillion required globally to achieve net-zero emissions, sovereign issuance can help kickstart these large capital inflows.[145] These issuances could be paired with initiatives to develop the domestic capital market (Box 4).

Box 4: ADB Support for COVID-19 and Other Labeled Bonds

In 2020, Thailand successfully issued an inaugural sovereign sustainability bond via its Public Debt Management Office (PDMO). This was the first sovereign sustainability bond issued in Southeast Asia. The bond, which was issued in taps, totaled THB197.0 billion (USD6.5 billion) as of 18 March 2022, according to the PDMO.

The sustainability bond framework is aligned with the International Capital Market Association's Sustainability Bond Guidelines and the ASEAN Sustainability Bond Standards. The bond issuance is part of a 15-year, benchmark bond program to be issued in the next 2 fiscal years in sectors related to green and sustainable infrastructure. The use of proceeds has both green and social components: the program finances green infrastructure through the Mass Rapid Transit Orange (East) Line Project; as well as social impact projects such as public health measures, job creation programs, and local public infrastructure development to assist with coronavirus disease (COVID-19) recovery and related social and environmental benefits. The green tap of the bond was certified against the Low-Carbon Transport Criteria of the Climate Bonds Standard. The Asian Development Bank (ADB) supported the Government of Thailand throughout this issuance by providing technical support on bond framework development, external reviews, and the development of systems to monitor the use of bond proceeds and prepare post-issuance reports.

continued on next page

---

[143] Climate Bonds Initiative. Green Bond Pricing in the Primary Market H1 2021. https://www.climatebonds.net/resources/reports/green-bond-pricing-primary-market-h1-2021.

[144] See https://www.economie.gouv.fr/budget-vert-france-1er-pays-monde-mesurer-impact-budget-etat-environnement.

[145] International Energy Agency. 2021. World Energy Outlook 2021. https://www.iea.org/reports/world-energy-outlook-2021.

Box 4 *continued*

In 2020, ADB also supported the National Housing Authority (NHA) maiden social bond, which was issued on 23 September in three tranches totaling THB6.8 billion (USD205 million). The NHA bond is among the first social bonds issued by a state-owned enterprise in Southeast Asia. The bond will finance affordable housing in Thailand and promote sustainable communities. ADB also supported the subsequent NHA social bond in March 2021 of THB3.0 billion and a sustainability bond of THB 2.1 billion in September 2021, incorporating green and affordable housing to the portfolio. Other green and sustainability bonds are under development. In 2020–2021, approximately USD5.6 billion was mobilized through these thematic bonds issued in Thailand with ASEAN Catalytic Green Finance Facility support.

Sources: Climate Bonds Initiative. 2021. *GIIO Thailand Report 2021*; ADB.

Unlabeled (Climate-Aligned) Universe

Methodology[146]

The unlabeled climate-aligned universe focuses on investment opportunities that are not explicitly labeled as "green" by the issuer, but nevertheless finance climate-aligned assets and activities. Bonds that are climate-aligned are identified at the issuer level:

(i)   bonds from fully aligned issuers that derive 95% or more of revenues from climate-aligned business lines, and

(ii)   bonds from strongly aligned issuers that derive 75%–95% of revenue from climate-aligned business lines

Identification of such instruments is critical for shedding light on capital flows financing green assets that are not as visible and transparent as labeled bonds, as well as identifying opportunities to expand the labeled green bond market.

Climate Bonds has identified eight climate themes: (i) renewable energy, (ii) transport, (iii) buildings, (iv) water, (v) waste, (vi) land use and agriculture, (vii) climate adaptation, and (viii) information and communication technology (ICT).

ASEAN+3 Context

With USD406.4 billion of climate-aligned outstanding bonds issued by 1,458 climate-aligned companies, the ASEAN+3 region accounts for some 44.5% of the overall climate-aligned universe. The PRC, the Republic of Korea, and Japan dominate this volume, with ASEAN-only nations thus accounting for just USD5.5 billion, or 0.6% of the global climate-aligned issuance. Thailand leads in the ASEAN issuance with USD2.6 billion of climate-aligned issuance across 52 issuers, followed by Indonesia with USD1.1 billion, the Lao PDR with USD997 million, Singapore with USD686 million, and Malaysia with USD54 million.

Thematic ASEAN+3 Climate-Aligned Universe Analysis

Transport dominates ASEAN+3's climate-aligned universe with 72% (USD293.3 billion) of climate-aligned bond issuance across 585 deals (Figure 20). China Railway Corp. is the top issuer, with a cumulative USD230.1 billion of aligned outstanding bonds, single-handedly accounting for 25% of the global climate-aligned universe and

---

[146]   The data on climate-aligned bonds is as of Q3 2020. Climate Bonds is working on updating this for Q3 2021, but at the time of writing the data were not yet available.

56.6% of ASEAN+3's climate-aligned universe. Energy is the second-largest climate theme and accounts for 21% of climate-aligned issuance (USD84.2 billion; 530 deals), the largest issuer being Korea Electric Power Corp. with USD25.3 billion of outstanding debt from 205 bonds. Buildings, water, waste, land use and agriculture, and ICT account for USD28.9 billion, or 7.1%, of ASEAN+3 climate-aligned issuance.

In ASEAN-only economies, issuance is more evenly balanced across sectors (Figure 21). Energy is the largest sector, with 29.3%, or USD1,607 million of climate-aligned issuance across 39 deals. The Lao PDR's EDL-Generation PCL is the largest issuer in the sector, with seven bonds totaling USD997 million of outstanding debt. Transport is the second-largest sector, accounting for USD1,605 million of climate-aligned debt across 26 deals. Thailand's Bangkok Expressway & Metro PCL, an issuer of sustainability bonds, is one of the largest climate-aligned issuers in the region and the transport sector, with USD630 million of unlabeled (conventional) debt due to mature before the end of 2025. Water and ICT are the next largest sectors, with USD1.7 billion and USD1.1 billion of outstanding climate-aligned bonds, respectively. Singapore's Hyflux Ltd. was the largest issuer in the water sector with its USD686 million issuance, but it has since been liquidated, leaving WHA Utilities and Power PCL as the largest issuer in the water sector with its USD246 million of outstanding debt. Land use and agriculture makes up just USD62 million of volume across four deals, while the waste and buildings sectors saw no issuance.

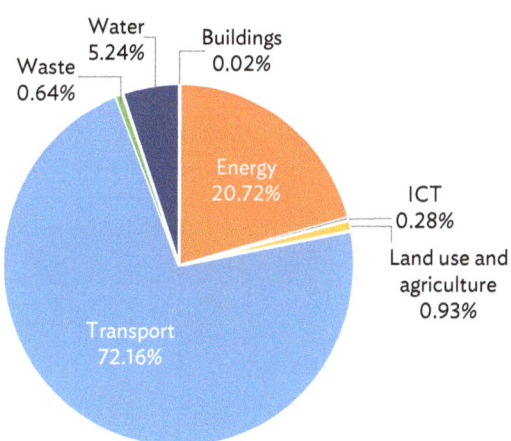

Figure 20: ASEAN+3 Climate-Aligned Issuance by Theme

Water 5.24%
Buildings 0.02%
Waste 0.64%
Energy 20.72%
ICT 0.28%
Land use and agriculture 0.93%
Transport 72.16%

ASEAN+3 = Association of Southeast Asian Nations (ASEAN), the People's Republic of China (PRC), Japan and the Republic of Korea; ICT = information and communication technology.
Source: Climate Bonds Initiative.

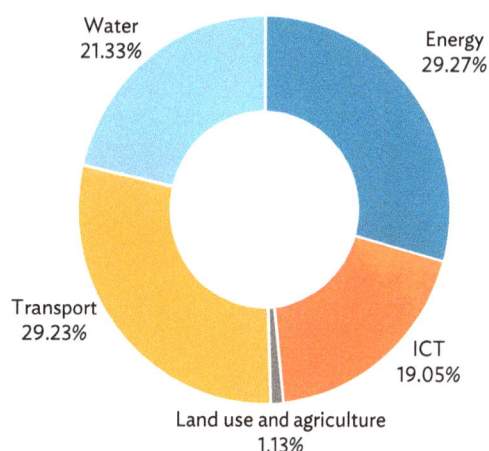

Figure 21: ASEAN Climate-Aligned Issuance by Theme

Water 21.33%
Energy 29.27%
ICT 19.05%
Land use and agriculture 1.13%
Transport 29.23%

ASEAN+3 = Association of Southeast Asian Nations (ASEAN), the People's Republic of China (PRC), Japan and the Republic of Korea; ICT = information and communication technology.
Source: Climate Bonds Initiative.

More than 50% of climate-aligned bonds issued in ASEAN mature within 5 years and 29% in 5–10 years. The water theme in ASEAN is skewed by Hyflux Ltd.'s USD686 million perpetual issuance but otherwise remains in line with other sectors, with 59.7% of issuance maturing in 5 years and 30.5% in 10–15 years (Figure 22).

CNY and KRW dominate climate-aligned debt in ASEAN+3, while THB, IDR, and SGD lead among ASEAN currencies (Figure 23). CNY is by far the most common currency of climate-aligned debt in the region, totaling 79.1% of the climate-aligned debt, followed by KRW's 13.9% share. Among ASEAN members, the split is more balanced, with 58.4% denominated in THB, 18.3% in IDR, 14.8% in SGD, and just 6.6% in USD.

Figure 22: ASEAN Climate-Aligned Issuance by Tenor and Sector

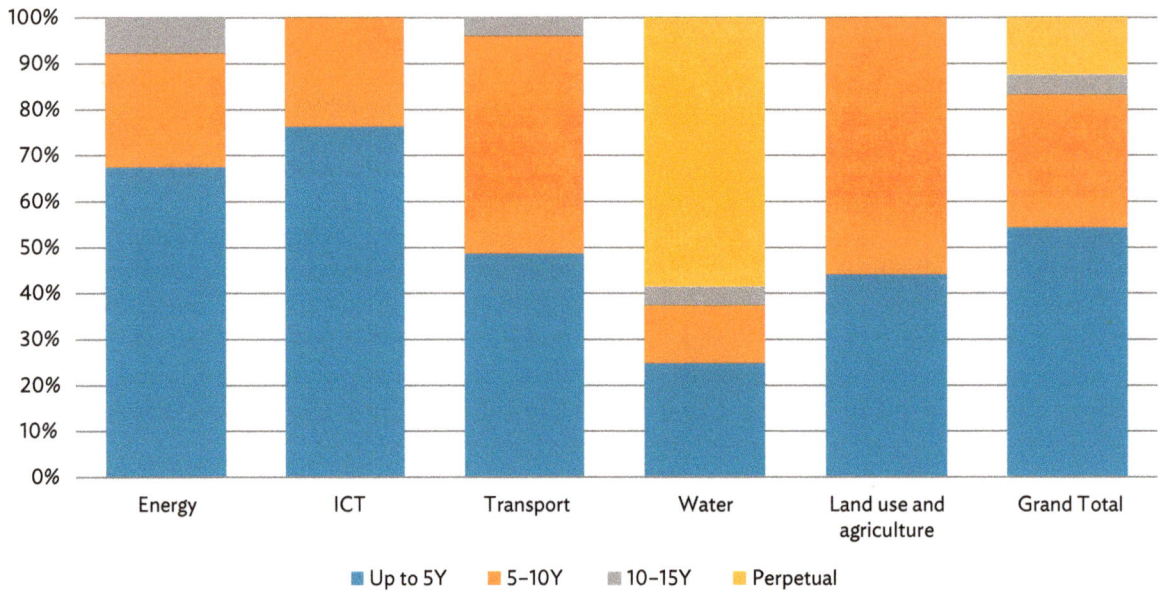

ASEAN = Association of Southeast Asian Nations, ICT = information and communication technology, y = years.
Source: Climate Bonds Initiative.

Figure 23: ASEAN+3 Climate-Aligned Issuance by Currency
(million)

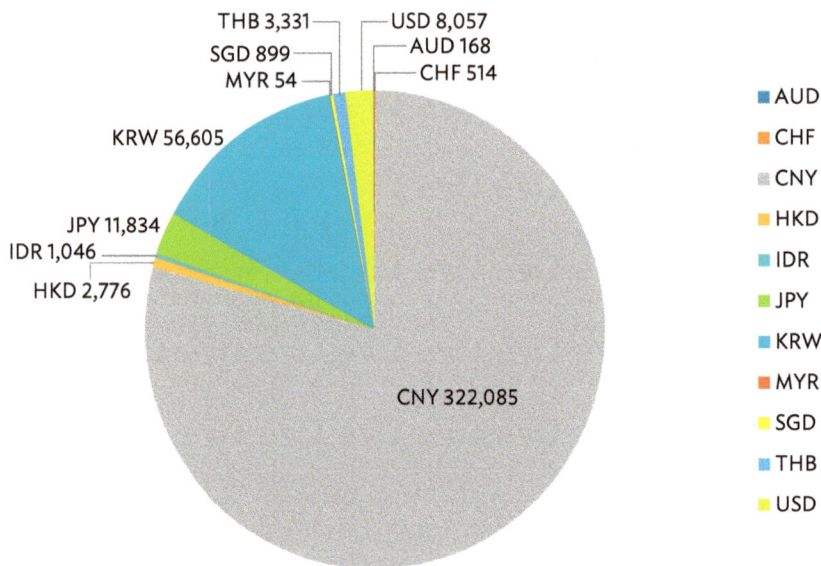

ASEAN+3 = Association of Southeast Asian Nations plus the People's Republic of China (PRC), Japan, and the Republic of Korea; AUD = Australian dollar; CHF = Swiss franc; CNY = Chinese yuan; HKD = Hong Kong dollar; IDR = Indonesian rupiah; JPY = Japanese yen; KRW = Korean won; MYR = Malaysian ringgit; SGD = Singapore dollar; THB = Thai baht; USD = United States dollar.

Source: Climate Bonds Initiative.

Opportunities exist to scale up ASEAN+3's labeled bond issuance. More than half (53.8%) of ASEAN+3's unlabeled climate-aligned bond issuance will mature by 2024. This highlights opportunities for climate-aligned issuers to refinance their debt with labeled green or sustainability bonds; given 95% of their revenues align with the taxonomy, it is likely that projects within these organizations are eligible to be financed using GSS instruments. Most opportunities come from the transport theme (USD151.3 billion of debt maturing with 5 years), followed by energy (USD50.0 billion) and water (USD12.4 billion). An additional USD90.6 billion will mature by 2029, providing more opportunities as those tenors draw closer, particularly for transport and energy theme issuers.

Some climate-aligned issuers have already entered the labeled green and sustainability bond markets. China Three Gorges Corp., the second-largest climate-aligned issuer in the energy theme and a leading hydropower operator, has tapped the green bond market. Other issuers who have utilized the labeled sustainable bond market include Hitachi Zosen Corp, Bangkok Expressway & Metro PCL, MTR Corporation Limited, and Edra Solar Sdn. Bhd.

Advisory Services for Issuers

Advisory services can help new issuers with limited experience in determining the types of projects and assets that qualify as sustainable finance, and how to structure a GSS issue. Private sector advisory firms are beginning to offer expertise in this space but may only be feasible solutions for new issuers if adequate subsidies are available. Development Financial Institution (DFI) are helping to facilitate the development of GSS instruments. For instance, ADB is providing technical assistance and advisory services for issuers in ASEAN+3 to facilitate GSS bond issuances as part of the ASEAN+3 Asian Bond Markets Initiative (Box 5).

Box 5: ADB's Technical Assistance to Provide Advisory Services for Issuers

The Asian Development Bank (ADB) is implementing a regional technical assistance (TA) program to develop ecosystem for sustainable local currency bond market development in ASEAN+3. Under the guidance of ASEAN+3 finance ministers and central bank governors, this TA was developed and implemented in accordance with the ASEAN+3 Asian Bond Markets Initiative's (ABMI) Medium-Term Road Map, 2019–2022. As a result, this TA program is truly owned by the ASEAN+3 governments. The TA's overall activities are overseen by the Thai Ministry of Finance's Fiscal Policy Office and the People's Republic of China's Ministry of Finance as co-chairs of Task Force 1 of ABMI.

This project aims to establish the necessary ecosystem for sustainable finance market development in the ASEAN+3 region. One of the key activities is to provide hand-on support to prospective issuers and underwriters to facilitate the issuance of sustainable bonds, from the identification of eligible projects, assets, and expenditures and preparation of green, social, sustainability bond frameworks, to discussions with external reviewers. Most recently, the TA assisted Thailand's Thaifoods Group (TFG) in launching the region's first social bond issued by a non-financial corporate issuer in accordance with ASEAN social bond standards.[a]

TFG is a complete food manufacture—in feed, farm, and food—specializing in poultry and pig production. Annual revenue for 2021 was THB35 billion (USD1.0 billion). The company operates in both Thailand and Viet Nam and has investments and operations in other areas relevant to the food industry such as innovation and the environment. Totaling THB1 billion (USD30.5 million) and with a maturity of 5 years, the bond was issued on 11 November under the ASEAN+3 Multi-Currency Bond Issuance Framework, which facilitates cross-border issuance of debt securities in participating markets. The Credit Guarantee and Investment Facility, a trust fund of ADB, guaranteed 100% of the bond, which was sold to leading Thai institutional investors.

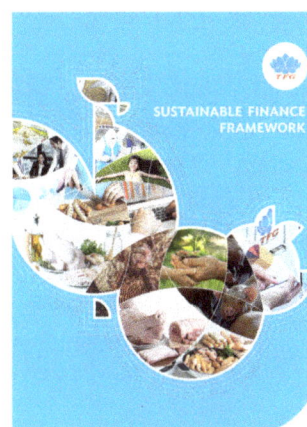

continued on next page

Box 5 *continued*

> More information can be found at the following websites:
>
> **TFG's Sustainable Finance Framework.** https://investor.tfg.co.th/misc/sustainable-finance/tfg-sustainable-finance-framwork.pdf.; External Reviewer's Report. https://investor.tfg.co.th/misc/sustainable-finance/tfg-social-bond-dnv-external-review.pdf.
>
> This technical assistance program is available to interested issuers wishing to issue sustainable local currency bonds in the ASEAN+3 region. For interested entities, please get in touch with Kosintr Puongsophol at kpuongsophol@adb.org.
>
> a   See First Social Bond Issued by Nonfinancial Corporate Issuer Under ASEAN Social Bond Standards, Asian Development Bank (adb.org).

Grant Schemes

Recently, several ASEAN+3 regulators and central banks are using grants to encourage sustainable finance flows. Malaysia's leadership by establishing the Green SRI *Sukuk* Grant Scheme (see Malaysia policy developments) providing tax exemption benefits for green *sukuk* issuers has led to similar developments elsewhere in the region. In November 2020, The Monetary Authority of Singapore (MAS) launched the world's first Green and Sustainability-Linked Loan Grant Scheme to support corporates obtaining green and sustainable financing.[147] Grants are capped at SGD100,000 (USD75,000) per loan over 3 years and intended to cover costs incurred in engaging sustainability advisory and assessment service providers. With the Government of Singapore providing new impetus, it is anticipated that sustainability-related products will continue to develop into 2022 and beyond. However, caution should be exercised with the KPI-linked model to ensure that the targets are sufficiently ambitious and consistent with global and science-based trajectories for decarbonization, as well as to ensure that verifiable progress is made over time.

In May 2021, the Hong Kong Monetary Authority (HKMA) announced the Green and Sustainable Finance Grant Scheme (GSF Grant Scheme) to strengthen Hong Kong, China's position as a regional green and sustainable finance hub.[148] The GSF Grant Scheme consists of two tracks: [149]

(i)   **General bond issuance costs.** This covers bond issuance expenses (e.g., arrangement, legal, audit, and listing fees) for eligible first-time green and sustainable bond issuers.

(ii)   **External review costs.** This covers transaction-related external review fees (e.g., including pre-issuance external review and post-issuance external review or reporting) for eligible green and sustainable bond issuers and loan borrowers, including first-time and repeated issuers and borrowers.

The grant amount for each green and sustainable bond issue is equivalent to half of the eligible expenses subject to a limit of HKD2.5 million (USD320,000) where either the bond, its issuer, or its guarantor(s) possesses a credit rating by a rating agency recognized by the HKMA, or HKD1.25 million (USD160,000) where none of the bond, its issuer, or its guarantor(s) possesses a credit rating by a rating agency recognized by the HKMA.

---

[147]   Monetary Authority of Singapore (MAS). 2020. MAS Launches World's First Grant Scheme to Support Green and Sustainability-Linked Loans. News release. 24 November. https://www.mas.gov.sg/news/media-releases/2020/mas-launches-worlds-first-grant-scheme-to-support-green-and-sustainability-linked-loans.

[148]   Hong Kong Monetary Authority. 2021. HKMA announces guideline on the Green and Sustainable Finance Grant Scheme (GSF Grant Scheme). News release. 4 May. https://www.hkma.gov.hk/eng/news-and-media/press-releases/2021/05/20210504-4.

[149]   See the Green and Sustainable Finance Grant Scheme (GSF Grant Scheme).

Green Project Pipelines

Key policy and institutional changes can help green infrastructure pipelines and associated green finance (including the green bond market) grow.[150] These measures help to raise the profile of green infrastructure, support critical finance channels for stakeholders in infrastructure development, diversify risks, and expand investor options.

Governments and policymakers should pursue the following measures:

(i) **Climate risk exposure should be factored into new infrastructure plans.** This would account for the future depreciation of assets as a result of changing precipitation patterns, rising temperatures, and extreme weather events.

(ii) **Adhere to international best practices and guidelines.** Consistency in definitions across borders is critical for attracting international capital flows. To avoid market fragmentation, policymakers should therefore leverage ambitious internationally accepted definitions of green.

(iii) **Increase public awareness of green infrastructure.** Green infrastructure investment pipelines can assist investors in recognizing that there is a sizable pool of financially attractive green investments.

(iv) **Modification of regulatory requirements.** This includes the promotion of a standardized approach to green tagging in project finance and the incorporation of climate-related criteria. Additionally, it could include the use of regulation and the mandate of national development banks to support climate-related infrastructure projects.

(v) **Educate the public about COVID-19 recovery bond programs.** Such bonds should be promoted through the issuance of green, sustainable, and/or blue bonds that support a more sustainable recovery and exclude activities that may become stranded as a result of climate policy changes or are resilient to climate-related physical risks.

Development Finance Institutions

(i) **Expand the use of blended finance to direct capital toward climate-related investments and activities.** This could include blended finance facilities backed by development banks, and include risk mitigation measures such as credit enhancement, guarantees, and currency hedging products.

(ii) **Encourage the disclosure of climate-related financial risks.** These examples include promoting the implementation of recommendations by the Taskforce on Climate-Related Financial Disclosures (TCFD) to bolster market confidence.

Issuers

(i) **Strengthen capacity through training on the definition of and guidelines for green bonds.** A better understanding of green definitions, taxonomies, and concepts can help issuers better assess future climate risks, resulting in increased green bond and *sukuk* issuance. Capacity-building efforts should prioritize institutionalized technical skill development over technical assistance from external consultants.

(ii) **Keep track of climate-resilience investments.** Accurate tracking of green bonds for climate resilience can assist investors in identifying available opportunities and directing capital flows toward resilience investments. It can assist government agencies in developing policy and regulatory guidance related to the labeling, issuance, and reporting of green bonds. Notably, tracking and reporting will help ensure the market's continued integrity.

---

[150] K. Davidson et al. 2021. *Green Infrastructure Investment Opportunities: Malaysia 2020 Report*. Climate Bonds Initiative. https://www.climatebonds. net/files/reports/cbi_giio_malaysia_20_03_bbd.pdf.

Investors

(i) **Increase the scope of green mandates.** Green mandates have been instrumental in accelerating the growth of the green bond market by providing a ready source of capital to invest in the growing supply of investment opportunities. Additionally, expanded mandates should take into account increased capacity to assess emerging market opportunities, such as those in ASEAN+3.

(ii) **Become involved in the creation and mediation of assets.** Discussions with governments should focus on the steps required to transition to a low-carbon economy and the capital required.

Demand Side

Expand the Investor Base

Aligning low-carbon and climate-resilient infrastructure with international definitions of green can facilitate attracting private overseas capital looking for green infrastructure opportunities. There is an increasing demand from institutional investors, particularly from members of the Organisation for Economic Co-operation and Development (OECD) and the PRC, for investment opportunities in Belt and Road Initiative economies that address environmental challenges and support sustainable development. This growing interest has resulted in the development and growth of dedicated green financial products including green infrastructure investment trusts and green index products that, thanks to the transparency of the assets financed, attract dedicated investors.

European investors have expressed interest in investing in emerging markets.[151] Global pension funds, such as those in Japan and Australia, are increasingly looking overseas for long-term investment opportunities. New approaches to interacting with larger investors may assist in achieving this goal. Reverse enquiries, in which an investor asks a bond issuer to issue a specific bond so that the investor can establish a long bond position in that borrower, is one example. It establishes a window for institutional investors to obtain the direct issuance of a green financial instruments. This lowers the transaction costs for both parties involved in the transaction.

Retail investment products like exchange-traded funds (ETFs) can also help to increase private sector participation. Retail investors having more access to GSS bonds could help to develop a more liquid market for these securities.

Central Banks Can Help to "Build Back Better"[152]

According to the Climate Bonds' report on *"Embedding Sustainability into the COVID recovery: A Primer for ASEAN Central Banks,"* central banks in the region, particularly in ASEAN countries ASEAN+3 central banks should establish transparent roadmaps outlining expectations for greening their financial systems. A critical component of these roadmaps, as recognized by the ASEAN central banks in their November 2020 report, is the generation of decision-useful information on financial institutions' exposure to environmental risks, in order for bank management, regulators, and other stakeholders to better understand and manage such risks. Incorporating sustainability objectives into risk management guidelines and disclosure requirements could be supported by changes to prudential regulation as discussed.

---

[151] Climate Bonds Initiative. Green Bond European Investor Survey 2019. https://www.climatebonds.net/resources/reports/green-bond-european-investor-survey-2019.

[152] Excerpt from Climate Bonds. 2021. *Embedding Sustainability into the COVID recovery: A Primer for ASEAN Central Banks.* https://www.climatebonds.net/resources/reports/embedding-sustainability-covid-recovery-primer-asean-central-banks.

(i)   COVID-19 compelled a number of central banks to postpone or adjust microprudential stress testing in order to alleviate immediate resource and regulatory pressures on financial institutions. However, it is critical for central banks to resume environmental stress testing in order to strengthen financial institutions' capacity and understanding. The French Prudential Supervision and Resolution Authority recently published the results of stress tests conducted on volunteer banks and insurers using climate scenarios developed by the Network of Central Banks and Supervisors for Greening the Financial System.

(ii)   In response to the pandemic, many central banks loosened microprudential and macroprudential regulations. Such adjustments can significantly boost credit availability to distressed sectors, for example, by releasing reserves from the countercyclical capital buffer. This can, however, inadvertently provide credit for potentially environmentally damaging activities that contribute to future climate risks. This risk can be mitigated by prohibiting sectors with high transition risks from accessing this newly released credit.

Regional central banks could also consider calibrating their monetary policy instruments, accounting for the climate-related risks of different bank assets.

(i)   Inappropriate use of indirect monetary policy tools such as open market operations and standing facilities may result in the accumulation of carbon-intensive assets, thereby increasing financial institutions' exposure to transition risks on their balance sheets. Changes to collateral frameworks have the potential to skew lending behavior and risk exposures.

(ii)   Direct monetary policy instruments used to stimulate economic recovery could be made more environmentally friendly. Corporate financing facilities, for example, in which the central bank purchases equity or debt directly from issuers, could also be skewed to promote green investment.

GSS Bond Exchange-Traded Funds and Indexes

Global ETFs saw net inflows of approximately USD639.8 billion in H1 2021, setting another record. Existing green bond ETFs contributed to 2020's strong growth, and two new funds were launched, including one for Canadian dollar investors, bringing the global total to eight.

Existing green bond ETFs are expected to continue to add assets, while new ones are expected to be introduced, reflecting increased investor awareness and preference for sustainable investments. Additionally, promoting ETFs and their corresponding benchmarks would give retail investors more investment options. Green bonds will face increased demand in both primary and secondary markets as a result of this.

Market Ecosystem

Guidance from Government and Regulators

The launch of the ASEAN GSS bond standards in 2018 and the *ASEAN Taxonomy for Sustainable Finance (Version 1)* mark a significant step in regional sustainable finance. Governments and regulators have started developing guidelines and regulations at the national level. These generally include guidance for issuance and disclosure in line with the GBPs and are mostly aligned with the Climate Bonds Standard. For instance, the People's Bank of China (PBOC) and the Financial Services Authority (OJK) in Indonesia have developed regulations for green bonds. These types of developments can be replicated across other countries to encourage further regional growth and can be supported by national strategies to promote GSS bond markets, similar to those found in the Bank of Japan's Strategy on Climate Change.

In the ASEAN+3 region, economies such as Singapore and Hong Kong, China have local organizations, securities regulators, capital market authorities, and central banks to provide support mechanisms to encourage GSS bonds issuance including grant schemes and other fiscal incentives. Other countries including Thailand have introduced waivers for approval and filing fees alongside reduced bond registration fees.

Mandatory Disclosure

Mandating disclosure and reporting around climate-related risks and opportunities can support informed capital allocation and encourage new capital investment. Introducing established standards and frameworks presents an opportunity to improve sustainability reporting and meet the disclosure expectations of GSS investors.

The TCFD recommendations are designed to increase the transparency, accessibility, and comparability of climate-related risks enabling investors to understand their investment portfolio exposures. Furthermore, green bonds are seen as an example of a climate-related opportunity in the TCFD Final Report Annex.[153] Following a drastic increase in 2021, close to 1,000 companies are now listed as TCFD supporters within ASEAN+3. Japan is one of the top five countries globally by the number of supporters and a clear leader in the region, followed by the Republic of Korea and Singapore. At the end of 2021, the HKMA and MAS were listed as central banks in support of the TCFD (Figure 24).

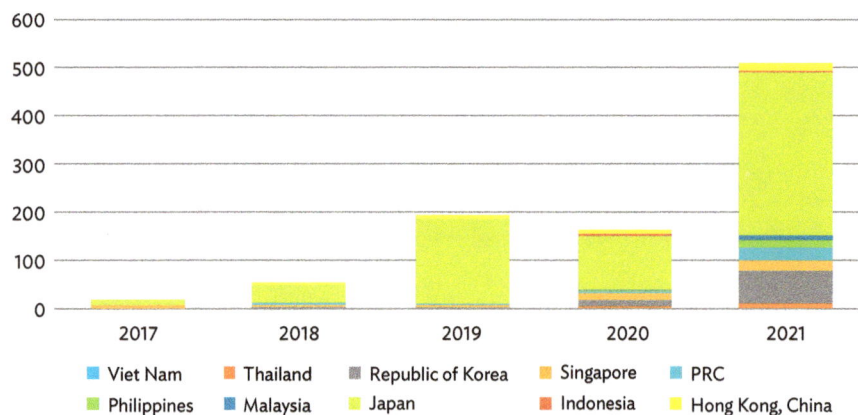

Figure 24: Taskforce on Climate-Related Financial Disclosures Supporters by Economy

PRC = People's Republic of China, TCFD = Taskforce on Climate-Related Financial Disclosures.
Source: TCFD Website.

Stock exchanges are actively promoting the TCFD in eight ASEAN+3 economies: Malaysia; Viet Nam; Indonesia; Japan; the Republic of Korea; Singapore; Thailand; and Hong Kong, China. The Singapore Exchange (SGX) has built on this by mandating all issuers to provide climate reporting on a "comply or explain" basis in their sustainability reports from 2022.[154] Similarly in Malaysia, the members of the Joint Committee on Climate Change are introductory mandatory climate-related financial risk disclosures based on the TCFD Application Guide from 2024. Following the announcement that TCFD-aligned climate-related disclosures will be mandatory across relevant sectors by 2025, the Stock Exchange of Hong Kong published guidance to listed issuers on climate disclosures to help companies assess their response to climate-related risks.[155] The Financial Services Commission in the Republic

---

153   Taskforce on Climate-Related Financial Disclosures. TCFD Knowledge Hub. https://www.tcfdhub.org/resource/icma-green-bonds-principles.
154   SGX Group. 2021. SGX mandates climate and board diversity disclosures. News release. 15 December. https://corp.sgx.com/media-centre/20211215-sgx-mandates-climate-and-board-diversity-disclosures.
155   HKEX. 2021. Exchange Publishes Corporate Governance and ESG (Climate Disclosures) Guidance. 5 November. https://www.hkex.com.hk/News/Regulatory-Announcements/2021/211105news?sc_lang=en.

of Korea is set to introduce mandatory ESG disclosure requirements for large companies from 2026 and all listed firms from 2030.

The Global Reporting Initiative offers a broader, alternate set of standards for organizations—large or small, private or public—to understand and report on their impacts on the economy, environment, and people comparably and credibly.[156] While the Global Reporting Initiative has a broader focus on ESG performance, several of the disclosures correspond, at least in part, to disclosures established in the TCFD recommendations.[157]

GSS and Sustainable Finance Platforms

In creating future pipelines, information on green assets and projects should be located in an easy to access, centralized location, like an online portal or platform that is available in multiple languages.[158] Improving visibility for infrastructure projects is a prerequisite for identifying the most effective green pipeline (Box 6). Accordingly, public-sector bodies in each country could establish a comprehensive database of infrastructure projects, listed by sector and status (e.g., tagged, planned, under preparation or ready to offer) and include other information and statistics for overseas investors including relevant disclosure information about sustainable bonds in their jurisdictions. Prospective issuers can also learn from examples and experiences of existing issuers in the ASEAN+3 region.

A single platform for ASEAN+3, such as ADB's *AsianBondsOnline*, could centralize these resources and serve as a knowledge hub for multiple stakeholders.[159] Corresponding platforms could also be created on a national level similar to the ThaiBMA.[160]

Box 6: Green Bond Transparency Platform

The Green Bond Transparency Platform (GBTP) is an initiative developed by the Inter-American Development Bank (IDB) to support green investments in Latin America and the Caribbean (LAC). The GBTP supports the harmonization and standardization of green bond reporting. The platform is taxonomy-neutral, accessible to everybody, and aims to provide a benchmark for best practice disclosure in the LAC region and beyond.

- For issuers, it facilitates reporting on the use of proceeds and impacts of their bonds in a simple format and standardized way, at both the project and project category level.
- For external reviewers, it provides a way to present their work with issuers (pre-and post-issuance) and the conclusions of these reviews.
- For investors, it enables analysis of the environmental performance and the use of proceeds of specific bonds.
- For public sector authorities, the GBTP is an evidence-based data tool to inform discussions on taxonomies and regulations.

Registered issuers and external reviewers receive free-of-charge assistance.

The GBTP was created in close cooperation with key international, regional, and local market players. Its data management, templates, and information have been piloted with over 40 market actors including issuers, investors, stock exchanges, standard setters, external reviewers, and certifiers.

Sources: Excerpt from Climate Bonds Initiative. 2021. *Cost Issuance Reporting in the Green Bond Market 2021*. https://www. climatebonds.net/resources/reports/post-issuance-reporting-green-bond-market-2021; Green Bond Transparency Platform.

---

[156]   Global Reporting Initiative. The global standards for sustainability reporting. https://www.globalreporting.org/standards.
[157]   Global Reporting Initiative. 2017. GRI's response to the FSB TCFD Report Consultation. https://www.globalreporting.org/standards/media/1379/item-10-submission-gri-tcfd-publication.pdf.
[158]   Climate Bonds Initiative. Green Infrastructure Investment Opportunities Indonesia. https://www.climatebonds.net/resources/reports/green-infrastructure-investment-opportunities-indonesia.
[159]   AsianBondsOnline. https://asianbondsonline.adb.org.
[160]   Thai Bond Market Association. Green, Social, Sustainability Bond & Sustainability-linked Bond. http://www.thaibma.or.th/EN/BondInfo/ESG.aspx.

6 | Summary and Next Steps

To deliver on international climate and sustainability commitments, sustainable finance can serve a critical role—as a complement to public money—in channeling private investment into the transition to a low-carbon, resource-efficient, climate-resilient, and inclusive economy.

Overall, the ASEAN+3 sustainable finance market continues to evolve in light of the pandemic and heightened attention on sustainability themes. Local currency (LCY) capital markets are at different stages of development across ASEAN+3 member economies; the legal and policy frameworks vary, as does the extent of current sustainable finance market development.

In Q3 2021, the regional cumulative sustainable debt market reached USD449 billion. At least one GSS instrument originated from the majority of ASEAN+3 economies. The LCY sustainable bond market grew around 50% each year from 2017 to 2019. In Q3 2021, half of the ASEAN+3 economies—the PRC, Japan, Malaysia, Singapore, and Thailand— had a majority of sustainable debt issuance in their respective domestic currency. Meanwhile, Hong Kong, China; Indonesia; the Philippines; the Republic of Korea; and Viet Nam had a majority of their sustainable debt issued in foreign currencies. The transition debt finance market in ASEAN+3 remains nascent with transition-labeled use-of-proceeds (UOP) bonds representing about USD1.7 billion regionally.

While supply has increased, demand for GSS bonds is growing all the time from a variety of sources. Greater investor understanding of climate risk, new fund launches, and a broadening market presence have all stimulated demand. Several regional policies and actions suggest continued progress in promoting LCY sustainable finance. Sustainable finance instruments can encourage further investment across ASEAN+3 economies when underpinned by GSS finance frameworks and clear issuance processes. The creation of transparent, sustainable financing approaches and instruments is fundamental to incentivizing investment as well as the transition to more sustainable practices.

As a next step, the recommendations below seek to promote the development of the GSS bond market in the ASEAN+3 region, taking into consideration the different levels of market development across economies.

Supply Side

(i) **Sovereign GSS bond issuances.** Emerging market sovereign issuance can channel green capital flows where they are most needed.

(ii) **Unlabeled (climate-aligned) universe.** These are investment opportunities that are not explicitly labeled as "green" by the issuer, but finance climate-aligned assets and activities.

(iii) **Advisory services for issuers.** Both public- and private-sector advisory services can support new issuers with limited sustainable finance experience in determining the types of projects and assets that qualify as sustainable finance and address misperceptions that GSS bonds carry considerably higher costs. These services could be institutionalized through a partnership between the government and a development partner, or via a government agency that makes such services accessible.

(iv) **Grant schemes.** Regulators and central banks can use grants to encourage sustainable finance flows.

(v) **Green project pipelines.** The growth of green infrastructure pipelines and associated green finance (including the green bond market) can be aided by key policy and institutional changes. International multilateral development agencies play a key role in blended finance, providing capital that mobilizes green or sustainable projects.

Demand Side

(i) **Expand the investor base.** Capitalize on increasing demand from institutional investors seeking sustainable investment opportunities.

(ii) **Central banks can help to "build back better."** Utilize the post-pandemic recovery toolkit used by central banks to protect ASEAN+3 member states from future systemic risks—particularly climate-related risks.

(iii) **GSS bond ETFs and indexes.** Increase awareness and investor participation toward investing sustainably.

Ecosystem

(i) **Mandates from government and regulators.** Securities regulators, capital market authorities, and/or central banks that provide support mechanisms can encourage GSS bond issuance.

(ii) **GSS and sustainable finance platforms.** Centralized information on green assets and projects should be made available in an easy-to-access portal or platform available in multiple languages.

APPENDIX 1
Economy Scorecards

For ease of comparison, the scorecards highlight current market situation in economies with green, sustainable, and social (GSS) bond issued.

People's Republic of China

Figure A1.1: People's Republic of China—Green, Sustainable, and Social Bond Scorecard

Country Profile	
Size of market (USD)	247.2 billion
Number of issuers	724
Number of instruments	1,209
Average size of instrument (USD)	0.2 billion
Median size of instruments (USD)	0.1 billion
Number of currencies	8
Average tenor (years)	15.5

Number of Issuances By Type and Year

Year	Pre-2019	2019	2020	<Quarter 3 2021	Total
Green	180	100	109	149	538
Sustainability	0	0	3	11	14
Social	0	0	3	1	4
Social-COVID-19	2	0	631	0	633
Sustainability-linked bond	0	0	0	19	19
Transition	0	0	0	1	1
Total	182	100	746	181	1,209

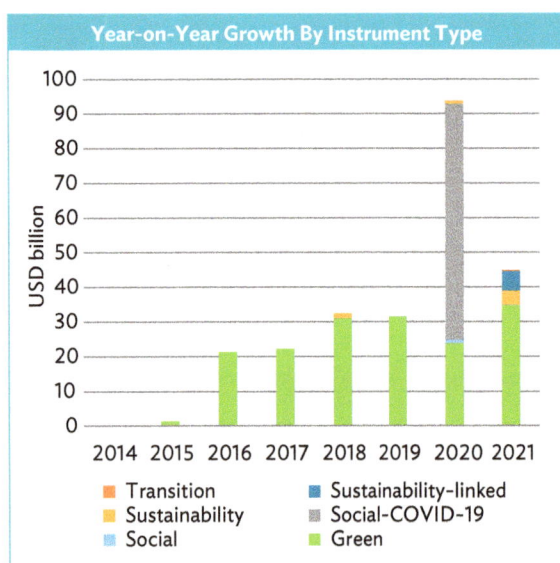

Year-on-Year Growth By Instrument Type

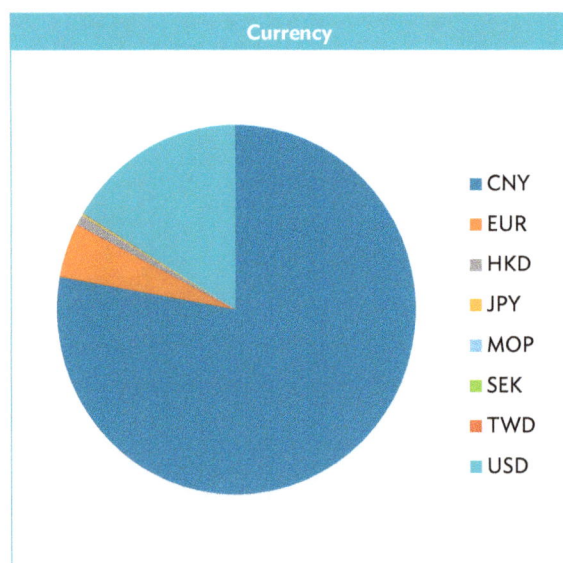

Currency

continued on next page

Figure A1.1 *continued*

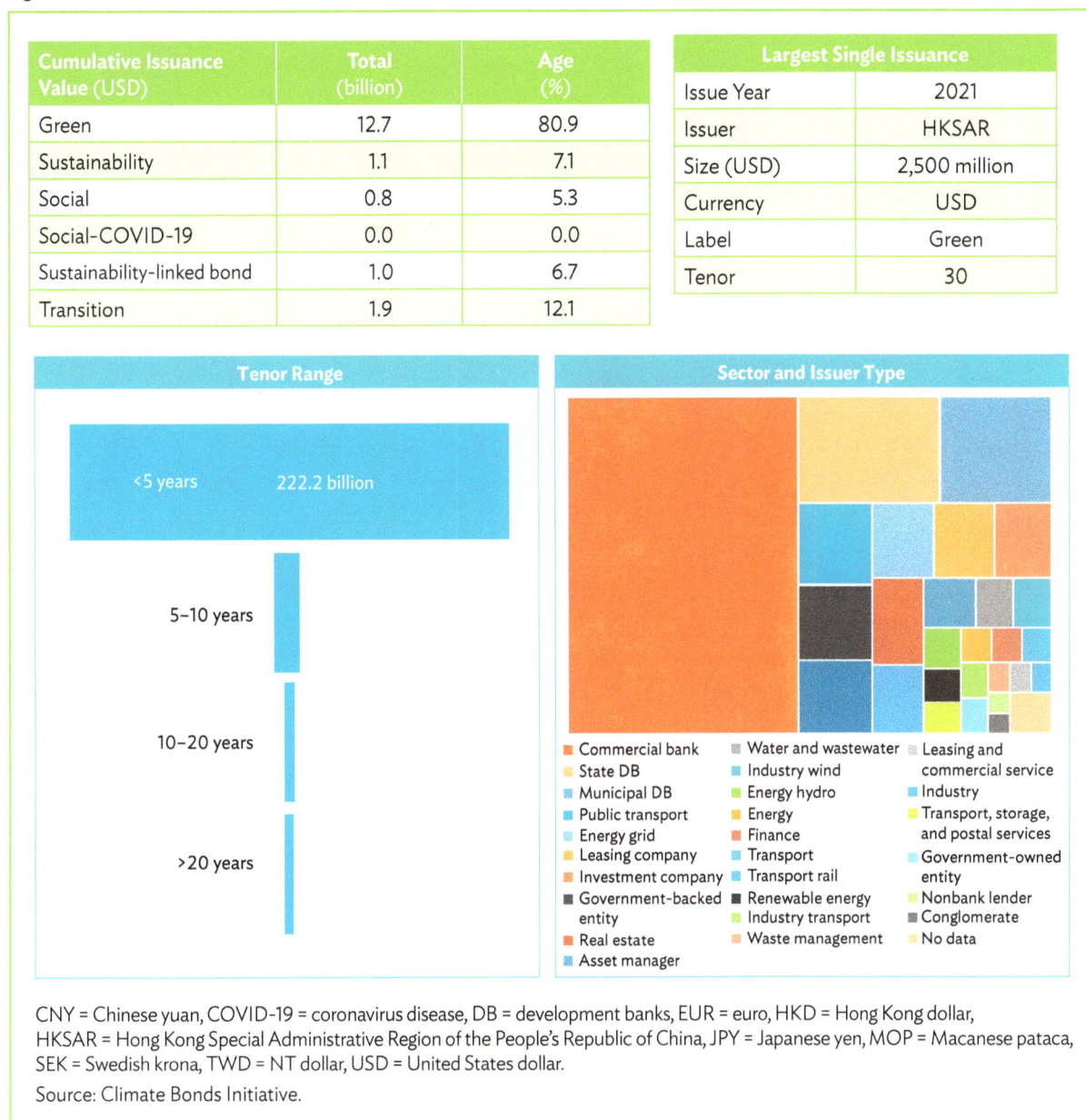

Cumulative Issuance Value (USD)	Total (billion)	Age (%)
Green	12.7	80.9
Sustainability	1.1	7.1
Social	0.8	5.3
Social-COVID-19	0.0	0.0
Sustainability-linked bond	1.0	6.7
Transition	1.9	12.1

Largest Single Issuance	
Issue Year	2021
Issuer	HKSAR
Size (USD)	2,500 million
Currency	USD
Label	Green
Tenor	30

Tenor Range

<5 years   222.2 billion

5–10 years

10–20 years

>20 years

Sector and Issuer Type

- Commercial bank
- State DB
- Municipal DB
- Public transport
- Energy grid
- Leasing company
- Investment company
- Government-backed entity
- Real estate
- Asset manager
- Water and wastewater
- Industry wind
- Energy hydro
- Energy
- Finance
- Transport
- Transport rail
- Renewable energy
- Industry transport
- Waste management
- Leasing and commercial service
- Industry
- Transport, storage, and postal services
- Government-owned entity
- Nonbank lender
- Conglomerate
- No data

CNY = Chinese yuan, COVID-19 = coronavirus disease, DB = development banks, EUR = euro, HKD = Hong Kong dollar, HKSAR = Hong Kong Special Administrative Region of the People's Republic of China, JPY = Japanese yen, MOP = Macanese pataca, SEK = Swedish krona, TWD = NT dollar, USD = United States dollar.

Source: Climate Bonds Initiative.

Hong Kong, China

Figure A1.2: Hong Kong, China—Green, Sustainable, and Social Bond Scorecard

Economy Profile	
Size of market (USD)	17.6 billion
Number of issuers	31
Number of instruments	77
Average size of instrument (USD)	0.2 billion
Median size of instruments (USD)	0.1 billion
Number of currencies	8
Average tenor (years)	14.7

Number of Issuances By Type and Year					
Year	Pre-2019	2019	2020	<Quarter 3 2021	Total
Green	26	9	16	6	57
Sustainability	0	0	0	5	5
Social	0	0	0	6	6
Social-COVID-19	0	0	0	0	0
Sustainability-linked bond	0	0	2	3	5
Transition	1	0	1	2	4
Total	27	9	19	22	77

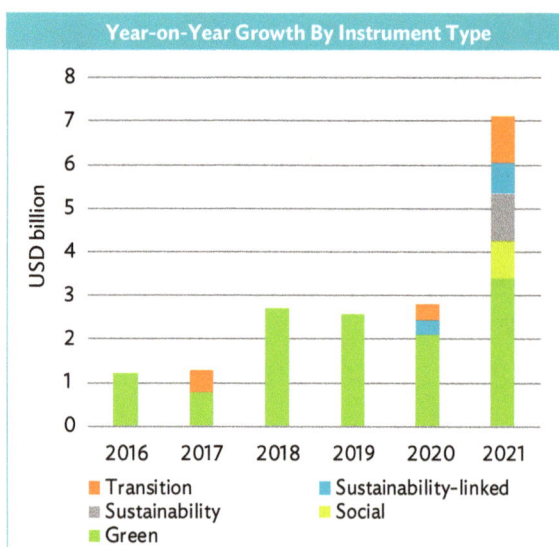

Year-on-Year Growth By Instrument Type

Legend: Transition, Sustainability-linked, Sustainability, Social, Green

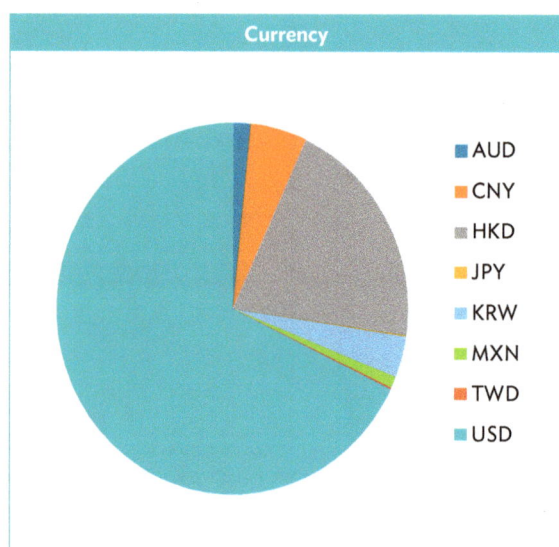

Currency

Legend: AUD, CNY, HKD, JPY, KRW, MXN, TWD, USD

Cumulative Issuance Value (USD)	Total (billion)	Age (%)
Green	12.7	80.9
Sustainability	1.1	7.1
Social	0.8	5.3
Social-COVID-19	0.0	0.0
Sustainability-linked bond	1.0	6.7
Transition	1.9	12.1

Largest Single Issuance	
Issue Year	2021
Issuer	HKSAR
Size (USD)	2,500 million
Currency	USD
Label	Green
Tenor	30

continued on next page

Figure A1.2 *continued*

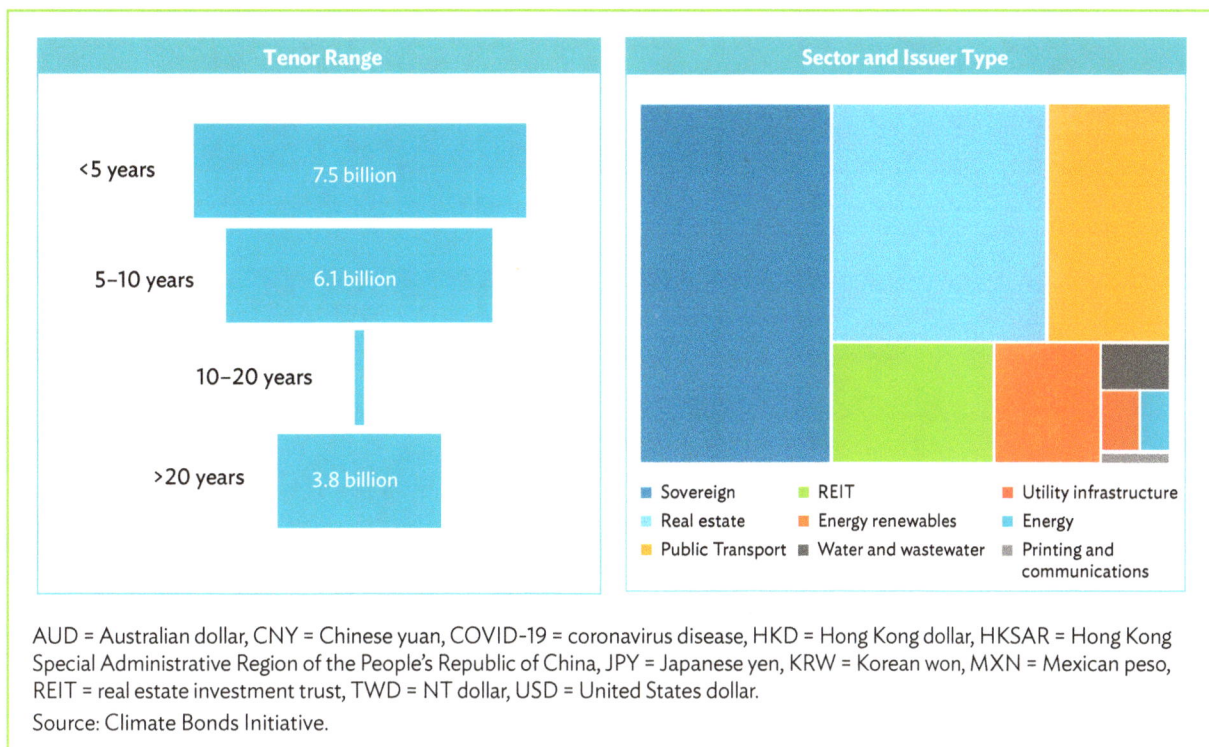

Tenor Range

<5 years	7.5 billion
5–10 years	6.1 billion
10–20 years	
>20 years	3.8 billion

Sector and Issuer Type

- ■ Sovereign
- ■ Real estate
- ■ Public Transport
- ■ REIT
- ■ Energy renewables
- ■ Water and wastewater
- ■ Utility infrastructure
- ■ Energy
- ■ Printing and communications

AUD = Australian dollar, CNY = Chinese yuan, COVID-19 = coronavirus disease, HKD = Hong Kong dollar, HKSAR = Hong Kong Special Administrative Region of the People's Republic of China, JPY = Japanese yen, KRW = Korean won, MXN = Mexican peso, REIT = real estate investment trust, TWD = NT dollar, USD = United States dollar.

Source: Climate Bonds Initiative.

Indonesia

Figure A1.3: Indonesia—Green, Sustainable, and Social Bond Scorecard

Country Profile	
Size of market (USD)	7.9 billion
Number of issuers	12
Number of instruments	18
Average size of instrument (USD)	0.4 billion
Median size of instruments (USD)	0.4 billion
Number of currencies	3
Average tenor (years)	21.4

Number of Issuances By Type and Year					
Year	Pre-2019	2019	2020	<Quarter 3 2021	Total
Green	4	1	5	2	12
Sustainability	1	0	0	2	3
Social	0	1	0	0	1
Social-COVID-19	0	0	0	0	0
Sustainability-linked bond	0	0	1	1	2
Transition	0	0	0	0	0
Total	5	2	6	5	18

continued on next page

Figure A1.3 *continued*

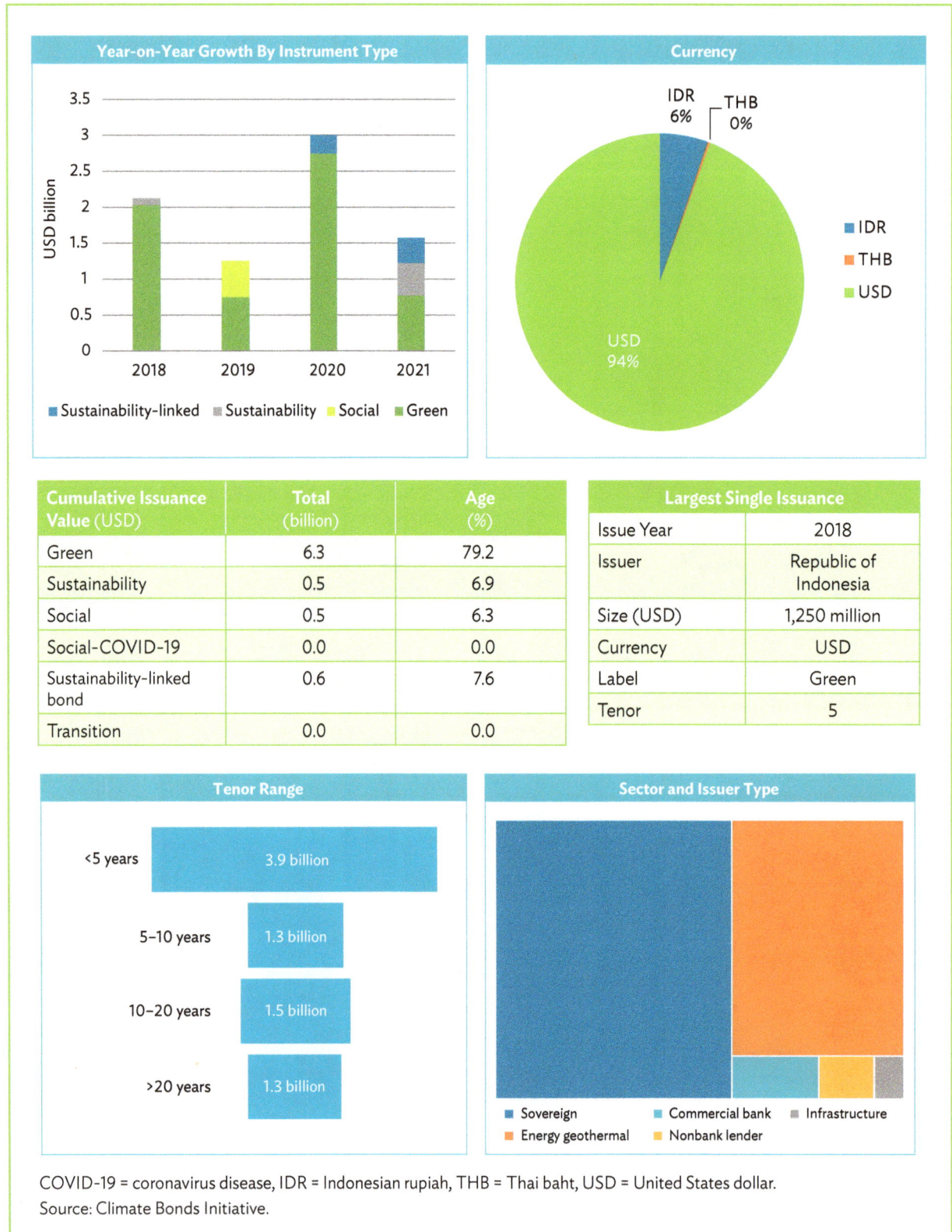

Year-on-Year Growth By Instrument Type

USD billion

2018, 2019, 2020, 2021

■ Sustainability-linked ■ Sustainability ■ Social ■ Green

Currency

IDR 6% THB 0%

USD 94%

■ IDR
■ THB
■ USD

Cumulative Issuance Value (USD)	Total (billion)	Age (%)
Green	6.3	79.2
Sustainability	0.5	6.9
Social	0.5	6.3
Social-COVID-19	0.0	0.0
Sustainability-linked bond	0.6	7.6
Transition	0.0	0.0

Largest Single Issuance	
Issue Year	2018
Issuer	Republic of Indonesia
Size (USD)	1,250 million
Currency	USD
Label	Green
Tenor	5

Tenor Range

<5 years   3.9 billion

5–10 years   1.3 billion

10–20 years   1.5 billion

>20 years   1.3 billion

Sector and Issuer Type

■ Sovereign   ■ Commercial bank   ■ Infrastructure
■ Energy geothermal   ■ Nonbank lender

COVID-19 = coronavirus disease, IDR = Indonesian rupiah, THB = Thai baht, USD = United States dollar.
Source: Climate Bonds Initiative.

Japan

Figure A1.4: Japan—Green, Sustainable, and Social Bond Scorecard

Country Profile	
Size of market (USD)	69.7 billion
Number of issuers	170
Number of instruments	422
Average size of instrument (USD)	0.2 billion
Median size of instruments (USD)	0.1 billion
Number of currencies	5
Average tenor (years)	11.2

Number of Issuances By Type and Year

Year	Pre-2019	2019	2020	<Quarter 3 2021	Total
Green	38	62	90	45	235
Sustainability	8	10	33	25	76
Social	10	20	43	27	100
Social-COVID-19	1	0	0	0	1
Sustainability-linked bond	0	0	3	5	8
Transition	0	0	0	2	2
Total	57	92	169	104	422

Year-on-Year Growth By Instrument Type

Currency

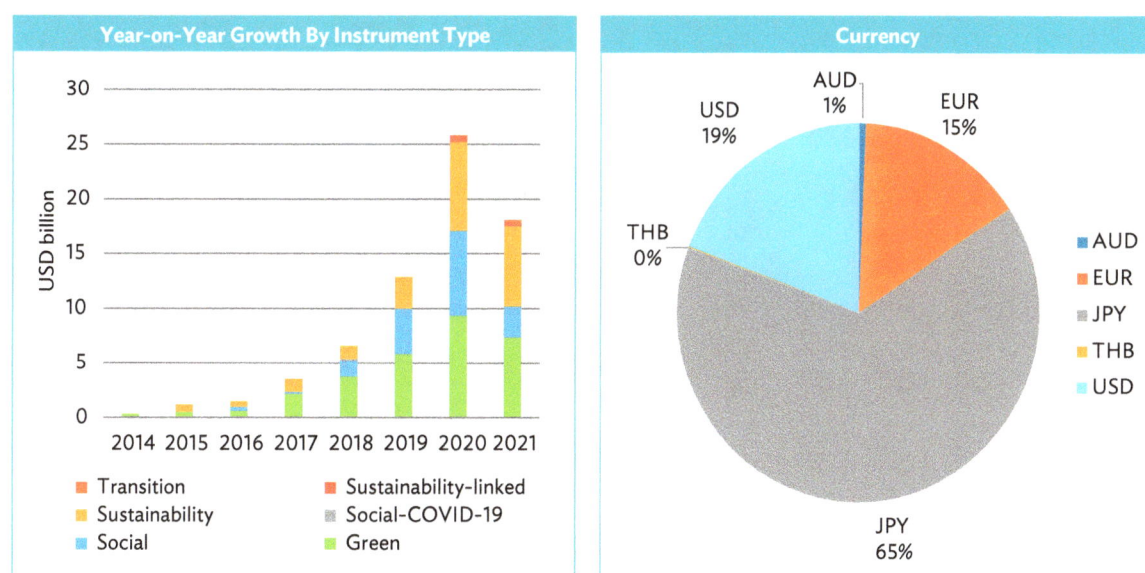

continued on next page

Figure A1.4 *continued*

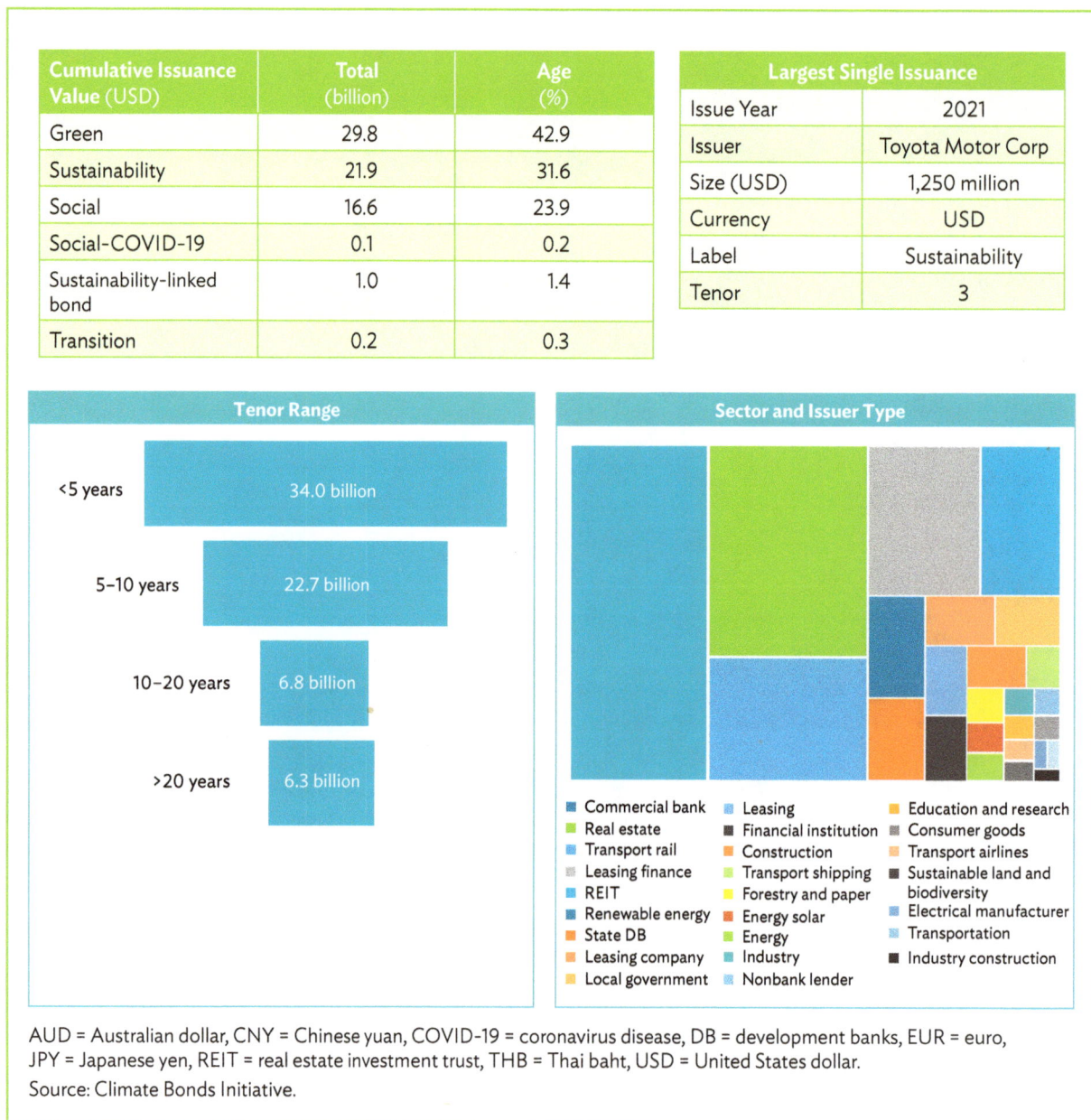

Cumulative Issuance Value (USD)	Total (billion)	Age (%)
Green	29.8	42.9
Sustainability	21.9	31.6
Social	16.6	23.9
Social-COVID-19	0.1	0.2
Sustainability-linked bond	1.0	1.4
Transition	0.2	0.3

Largest Single Issuance	
Issue Year	2021
Issuer	Toyota Motor Corp
Size (USD)	1,250 million
Currency	USD
Label	Sustainability
Tenor	3

Tenor Range

- <5 years: 34.0 billion
- 5–10 years: 22.7 billion
- 10–20 years: 6.8 billion
- >20 years: 6.3 billion

Sector and Issuer Type

- Commercial bank
- Real estate
- Transport rail
- Leasing finance
- REIT
- Renewable energy
- State DB
- Leasing company
- Local government
- Leasing
- Financial institution
- Construction
- Transport shipping
- Forestry and paper
- Energy solar
- Energy
- Industry
- Nonbank lender
- Education and research
- Consumer goods
- Transport airlines
- Sustainable land and biodiversity
- Electrical manufacturer
- Transportation
- Industry construction

AUD = Australian dollar, CNY = Chinese yuan, COVID-19 = coronavirus disease, DB = development banks, EUR = euro, JPY = Japanese yen, REIT = real estate investment trust, THB = Thai baht, USD = United States dollar.

Source: Climate Bonds Initiative.

Republic of Korea

Figure A1.5: Republic of Korea—Green, Sustainable, and Social Bond Scorecard

Country Profile	
Size of market (USD)	68.5 billion
Number of issuers	89
Number of instruments	384
Average size of instrument (USD)	0.2 billion
Median size of instruments (USD)	0.1 billion
Number of currencies	9
Average tenor (years)	5.0

Number of Issuances By Type and Year					
Year	Pre-2019	2019	2020	<Quarter 3 2021	Total
Green	11	9	10	32	62
Sustainability	8	17	39	98	162
Social	6	15	68	68	157
Social-COVID-19	0	0	3	0	3
Sustainability-linked bond	0	0	0	0	0
Transition	0	0	0	0	0
Total	25	41	120	198	384

Year-on-Year Growth By Instrument Type

Currency

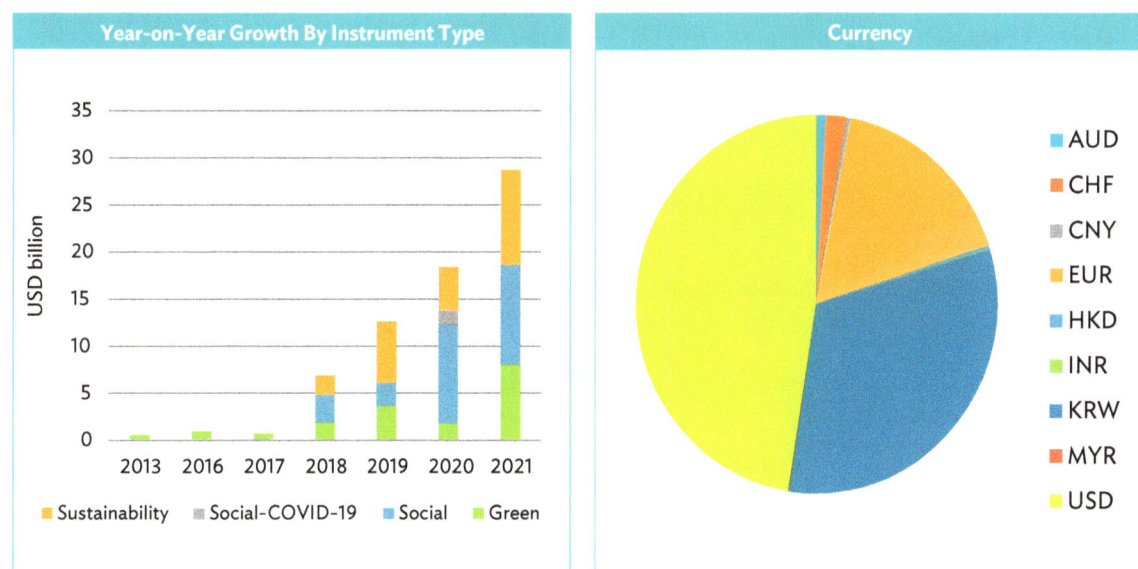

continued on next page

Figure A1.5 *continued*

Cumulative Issuance Value (USD)	Total (billion)	Age (%)
Green	17.3	25.2
Sustainability	23.3	34.0
Social	26.4	38.6
Social-COVID-19	1.5	2.2
Sustainability-linked bond	0.0	0.0
Transition	0.0	0.0

Largest Single Issuance	
Issue Year	2021
Issuer	Toyota Motor Corp
Size (USD)	1,250 million
Currency	USD
Label	Sustainability
Tenor	3

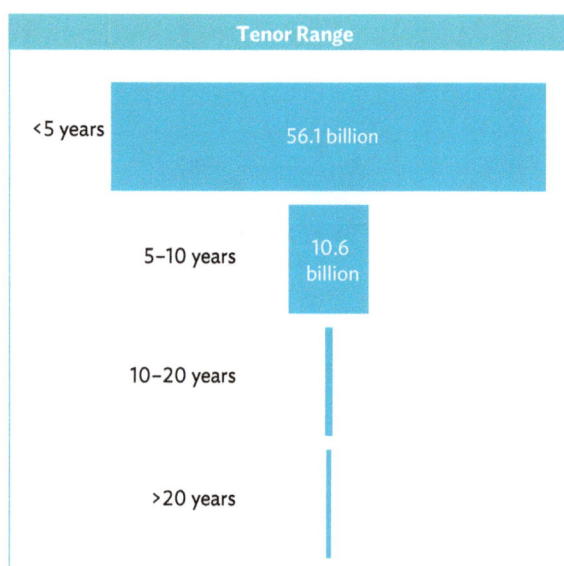

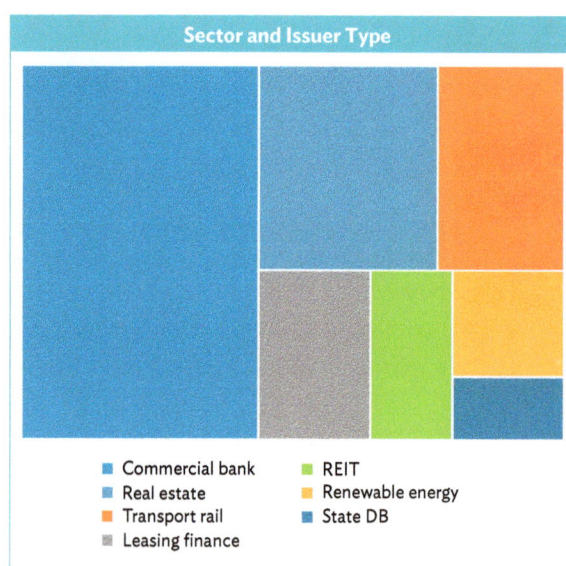

Tenor Range

<5 years	56.1 billion
5–10 years	10.6 billion
10–20 years	
>20 years	

Sector and Issuer Type

- Commercial bank
- Real estate
- Transport rail
- Leasing finance
- REIT
- Renewable energy
- State DB

AUD = Australian dollar, CHF = Swiss franc, CNY = Chinese yuan, COVID-19 = coronavirus disease, DB = development banks, EUR = euro, HKD = Hong Kong dollar, INR = Indian rupee, KRW = Korean won, MYR = Malaysian ringgit, REIT = real estate investment trust, USD = United States dollar.
Source: Climate Bonds Initiative.

Malaysia

Figure A1.6: Malaysia—Green, Sustainable, and Social Bond Scorecard

Country Profile	
Size of market (USD)	4.5 billion
Number of issuers	21
Number of instruments	47
Average size of instrument (USD)	0.1 billion
Median size of instruments (USD)	0.1 billion
Number of currencies	2
Average tenor (years)	11.3

Number of Issuances By Type and Year

Year	Pre-2019	2019	2020	<Quarter 3 2021	Total
Green	6	4	3	3	16
Sustainability	2	12	6	11	31
Social	0	0	0	0	0
Social-COVID-19	0	0	0	0	0
Sustainability-linked bond	0	0	0	0	0
Transition	0	0	0	0	0
Total	8	16	9	14	47

Year-on-Year Growth By Instrument Type

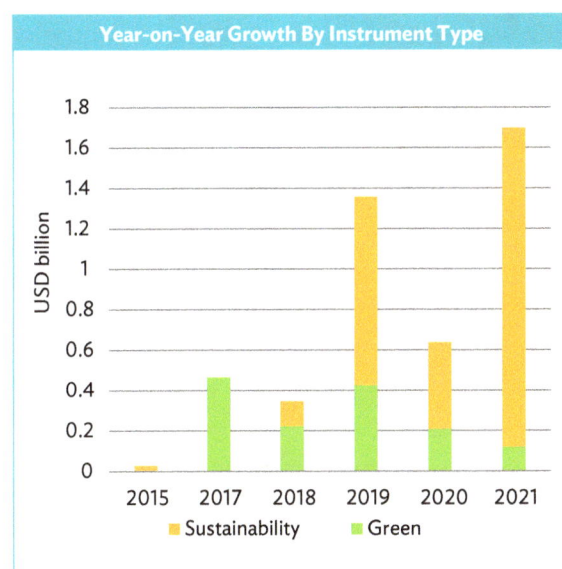

Currency

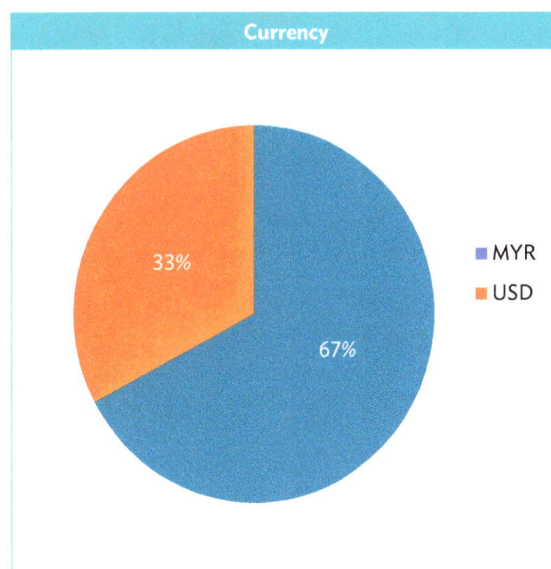

continued on next page

Figure A1.6 *continued*

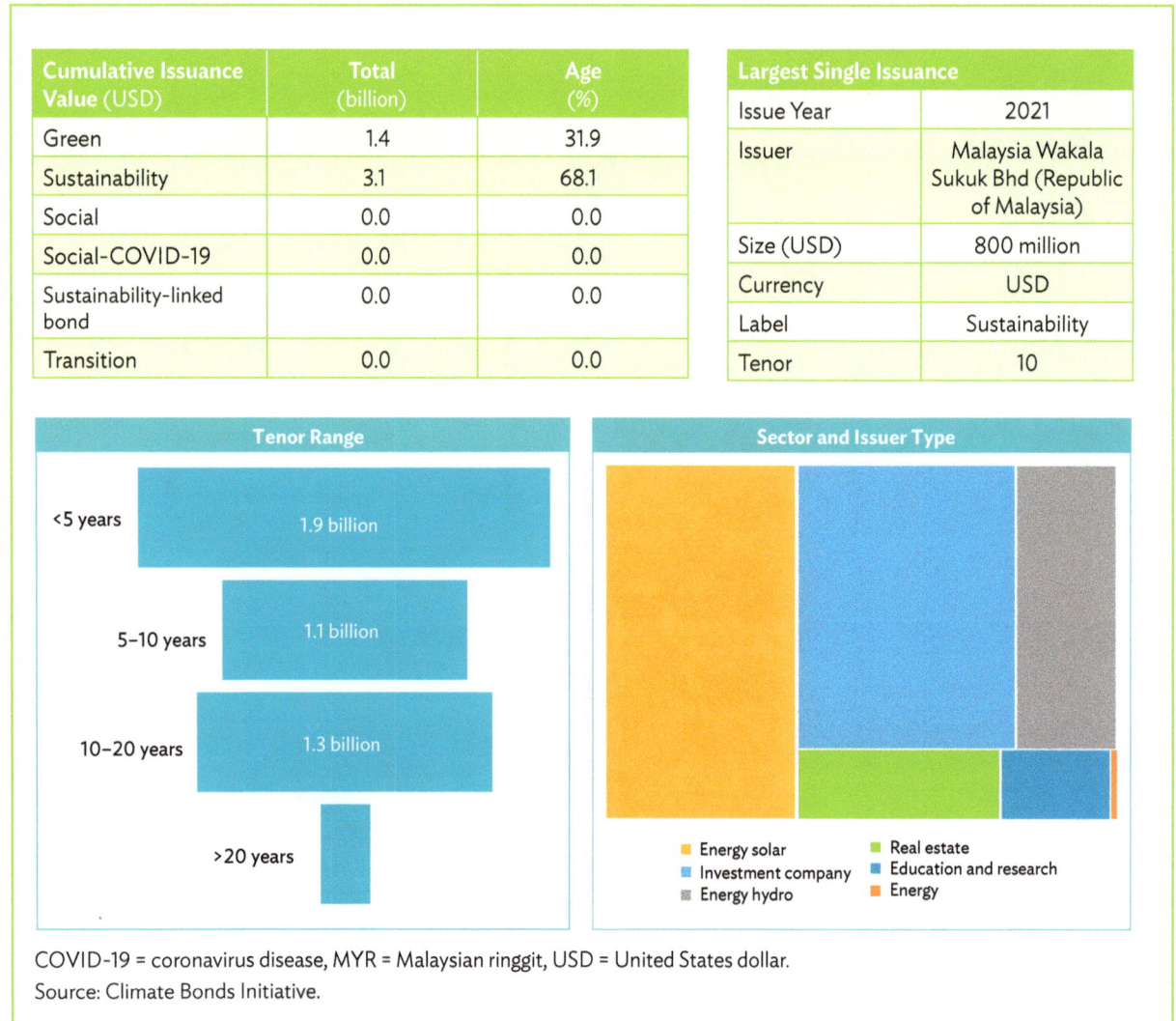

Cumulative Issuance Value (USD)	Total (billion)	Age (%)
Green	1.4	31.9
Sustainability	3.1	68.1
Social	0.0	0.0
Social-COVID-19	0.0	0.0
Sustainability-linked bond	0.0	0.0
Transition	0.0	0.0

Largest Single Issuance	
Issue Year	2021
Issuer	Malaysia Wakala Sukuk Bhd (Republic of Malaysia)
Size (USD)	800 million
Currency	USD
Label	Sustainability
Tenor	10

Tenor Range

- <5 years: 1.9 billion
- 5–10 years: 1.1 billion
- 10–20 years: 1.3 billion
- >20 years

Sector and Issuer Type

- Energy solar
- Investment company
- Energy hydro
- Real estate
- Education and research
- Energy

COVID-19 = coronavirus disease, MYR = Malaysian ringgit, USD = United States dollar.
Source: Climate Bonds Initiative.

Philippines

Figure A1.7: Philippines—Green, Sustainable, and Social Bond Scorecard

Country Profile	
Size of market (USD)	6.1 billion
Number of issuers	12
Number of instruments	27
Average size of instrument (USD)	0.2 billion
Median size of instruments (USD)	0.2 billion
Number of currencies	3
Average tenor (years)	13.6

Number of Issuances By Type and Year					
Year	Pre-2019	2019	2020	‹Quarter 3 2021	Total
Green	3	7	4	3	17
Sustainability	0	4	3	2	9
Social	0	0	1	0	1
Social-COVID-19	0	0	0	0	0
Sustainability-linked bond	0	0	0	0	0
Transition	0	0	0	0	0
Total	3	11	8	5	27

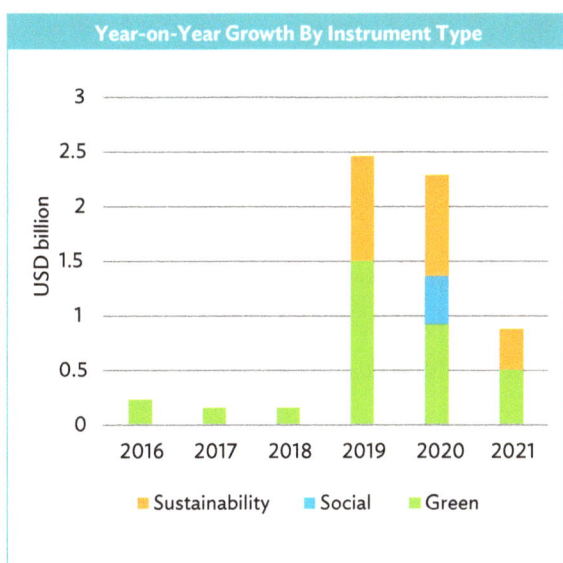

Year-on-Year Growth By Instrument Type

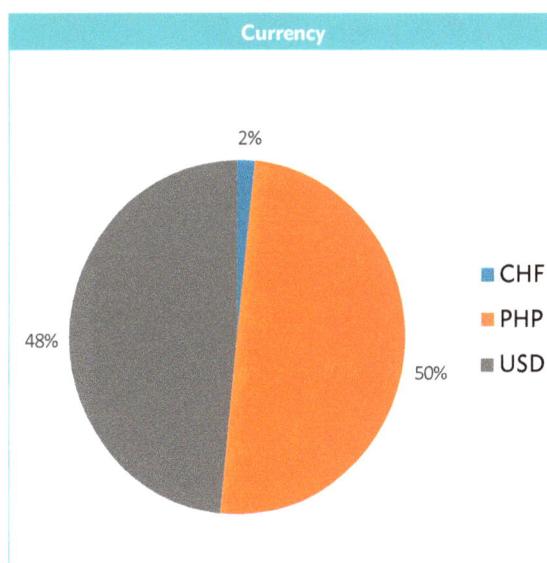

Currency

continued on next page

Figure A1.7 *continued*

Cumulative Issuance Value (USD)	Total (billion)	Age (%)
Green	3.4	56.1
Sustainability	2.3	36.7
Social	0.4	7.2
Social-COVID-19	0.0	0.0
Sustainability-linked bond	0.0	0.0
Transition	0.0	0.0

Largest Single Issuance	
Issue Year	2020
Issuer	Manila Water (Ayala Corporation)
Size (USD)	30,000 million
Currency	USD
Label	Green
Tenor	10

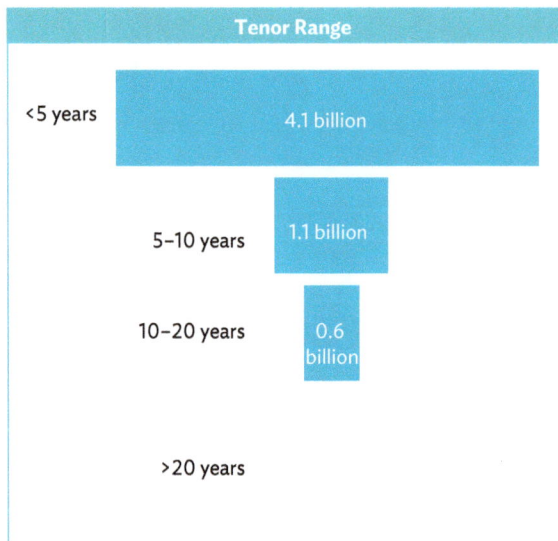

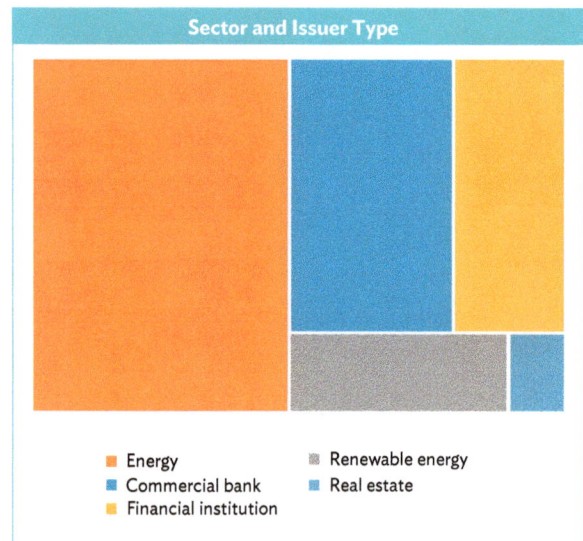

Tenor Range

- <5 years — 4.1 billion
- 5–10 years — 1.1 billion
- 10–20 years — 0.6 billion
- >20 years

Sector and Issuer Type

- Energy
- Commercial bank
- Financial institution
- Renewable energy
- Real estate

CHF = Swiss franc, COVID-19 = coronavirus disease, PHP = Philippine peso, USD = United States dollar.
Source: Climate Bonds Initiative.

Singapore

Figure A1.8: Singapore—Green, Sustainable, and Social Bond Scorecard

Country Profile	
Size of market (USD)	6.1 billion
Number of issuers	12
Number of instruments	27
Average size of instrument (USD)	0.2 billion
Median size of instruments (USD)	0.2 billion
Number of currencies	3
Average tenor (years)	13.6

Number of Issuances By Type and Year					
Year	Pre-2019	2019	2020	<Quarter 3 2021	Total
Green	3	7	4	3	17
Sustainability	0	4	3	2	9
Social	0	0	1	0	1
Social-COVID-19	0	0	0	0	0
Sustainability-linked bond	0	0	0	0	0
Transition	0	0	0	0	0
Total	3	11	8	5	27

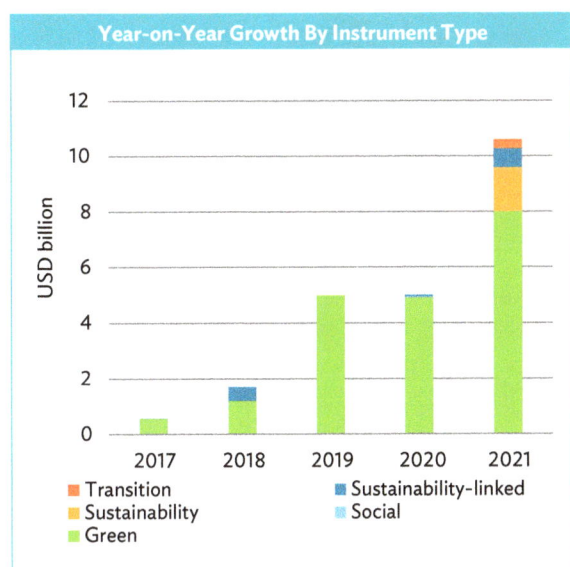

Year-on-Year Growth By Instrument Type

- Transition
- Sustainability
- Green
- Sustainability-linked
- Social

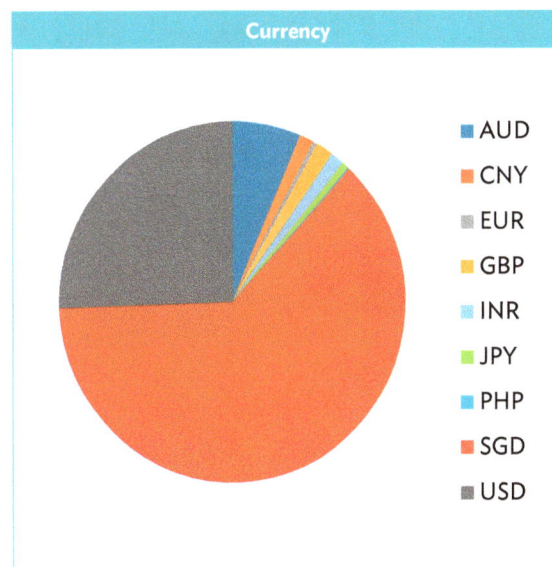

Currency

- AUD
- CNY
- EUR
- GBP
- INR
- JPY
- PHP
- SGD
- USD

continued on next page

Figure A1.8 *continued*

Cumulative Issuance Value (USD)	Total (billion)	Age (%)
Green	19.6	87.2
Sustainability	1.6	7.0
Social	0.0	0.2
Social-COVID-19	0.0	0.0
Sustainability-linked bond	1.3	5.6
Transition	0.3	1.4

Largest Single Issuance	
Issue Year	2021
Issuer	National Energy Agency
Size (USD)	969 million
Currency	SGD
Label	Green
Tenor	30

Tenor Range

<5 years	18.6 billion
5–10 years	
10–20 years	
>20 years	

Sector and Issuer Type

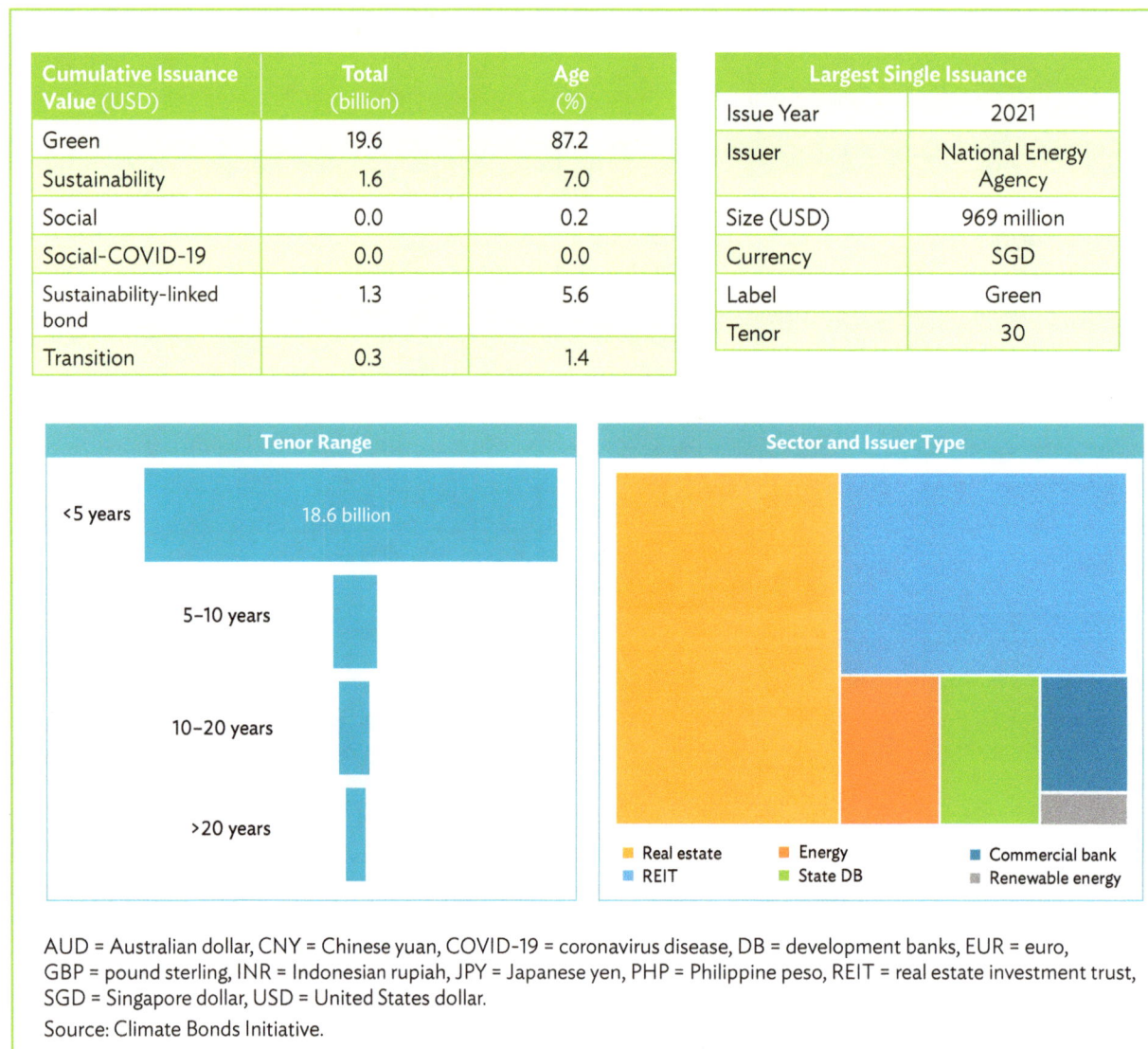

- Real estate
- REIT
- Energy
- State DB
- Commercial bank
- Renewable energy

AUD = Australian dollar, CNY = Chinese yuan, COVID-19 = coronavirus disease, DB = development banks, EUR = euro, GBP = pound sterling, INR = Indonesian rupiah, JPY = Japanese yen, PHP = Philippine peso, REIT = real estate investment trust, SGD = Singapore dollar, USD = United States dollar.

Source: Climate Bonds Initiative.

Thailand

Figure A1.9: Thailand—Green, Sustainable, and Social Bond Scorecard

Country Profile	
Size of market (USD)	8.8 billion
Number of issuers	9
Number of instruments	37
Average size of instrument (USD)	0.2 billion
Median size of instruments (USD)	0.1 billion
Number of currencies	2
Average tenor (years)	9.5

Number of Issuances By Type and Year

Year	Pre-2019	2019	2020	<Quarter 3 2021	Total
Green	2	4	6	6	18
Sustainability	1	0	3	10	14
Social	0	0	3	1	4
Social-COVID-19	0	0	0	0	0
Sustainability-linked bond	0	0	0	1	1
Transition	0	0	0	0	0
Total	3	4	12	18	37

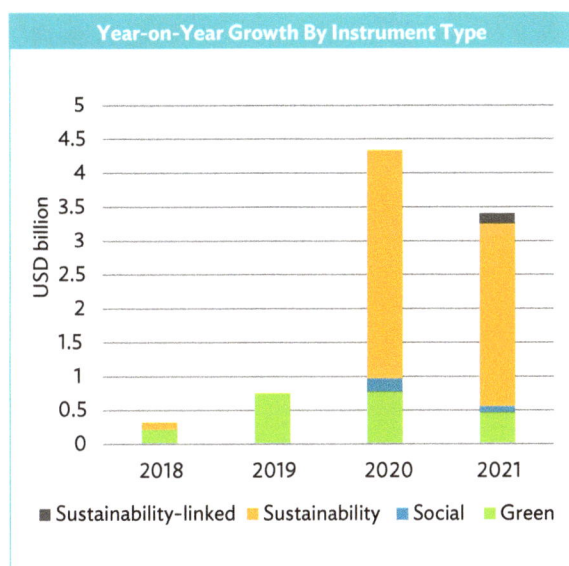

Year-on-Year Growth By Instrument Type

■ Sustainability-linked ■ Sustainability ■ Social ■ Green

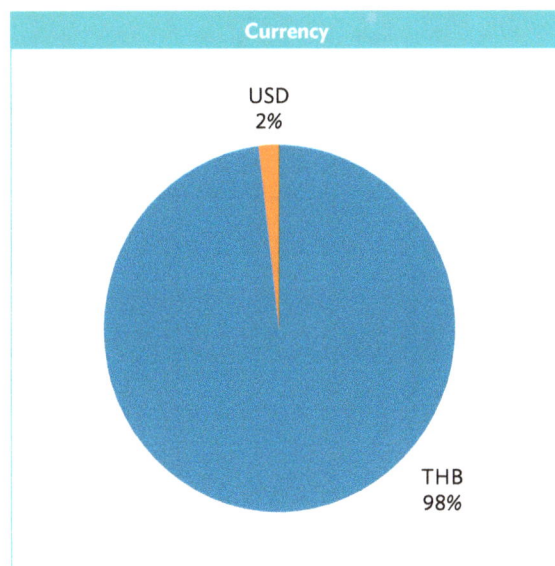

Currency

USD 2%

THB 98%

continued on next page

Figure A1.9 *continued*

Cumulative Issuance Value (USD)	Total (billion)	Age (%)
Green	2.2	24.7
Sustainability	6.2	70.2
Social	0.3	3.4
Social-COVID-19	0.0	0.0
Sustainability-linked bond	0.2	1.7
Transition	0.0	0.0

Largest Single Issuance	
Issue Year	2020
Issuer	Thailand Government Bond
Size (USD)	65,000 million
Currency	THB
Label	Sustainability
Tenor	15.32777778

Tenor Range

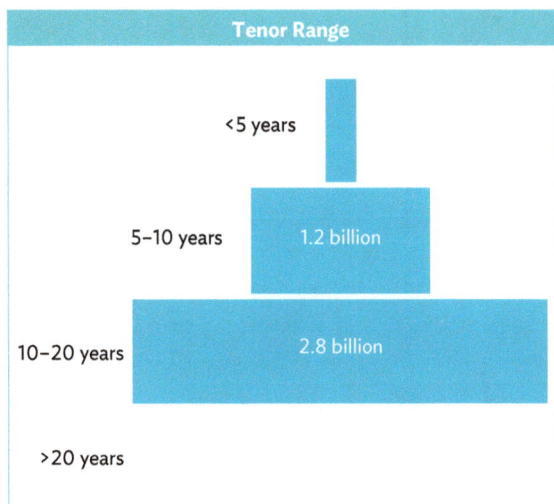

- <5 years
- 5–10 years — 1.2 billion
- 10–20 years — 2.8 billion
- >20 years

Sector and Issuer Type

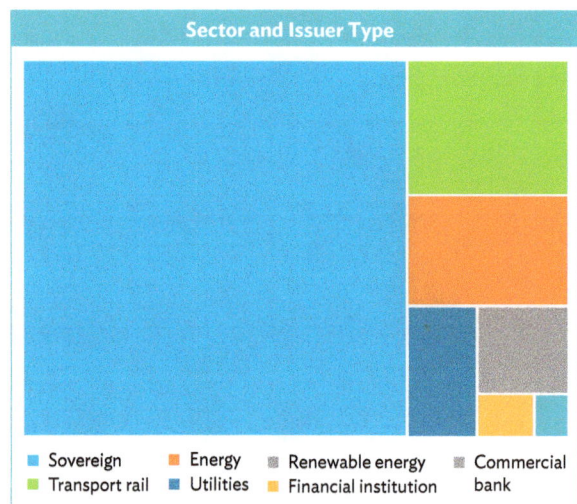

- Sovereign
- Transport rail
- Energy
- Utilities
- Renewable energy
- Financial institution
- Commercial bank

COVID-19 = coronavirus disease, THB = Thai baht, USD = United States dollar.
Source: Climate Bonds Initiative.

Viet Nam

Figure A1.10: Viet Nam—Green, Sustainable, and Social Bond Scorecard

Country Profile	
Size of market (USD)	0.7 billion
Number of issuers	6
Number of instruments	6
Average size of instrument (USD)	0.1 billion
Median size of instruments (USD)	0.1 billion
Number of currencies	2
Average tenor (years)	7.5

Number of Issuances By Type and Year

Year	Pre-2019	2019	2020	<Quarter 3 2021	Total
Green	2	1	2	1	6
Sustainability	0	0	0	0	0
Social	0	0	0	0	0
Social-COVID-19	0	0	0	0	0
Sustainability-linked bond	0	0	0	0	0
Transition	0	0	0	0	0
Total	2	1	2	1	6

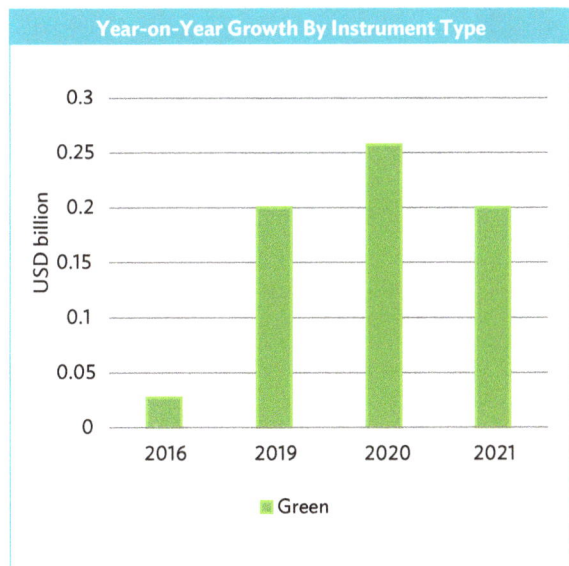

Year-on-Year Growth By Instrument Type

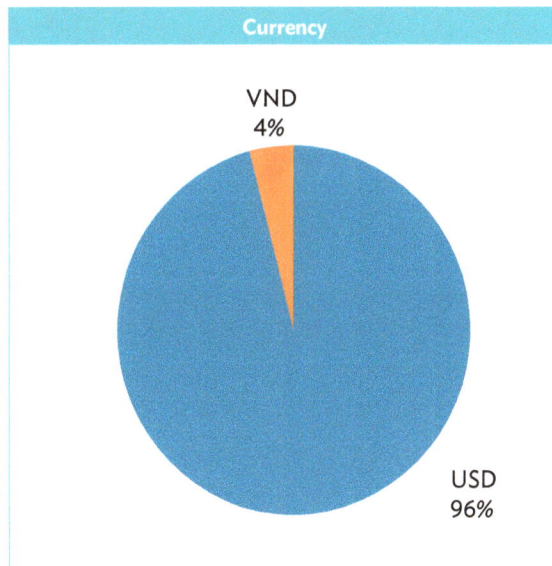

Currency

continued on next page

Figure A1.10 *continued*

Cumulative Issuance Value (USD)	Total (million)	Age (%)
Green	683.85	100.0
Sustainability	0.00	0.0
Social	0.00	0.0
Social-COVID-19	0.00	0.0
Sustainability-linked bond	0.00	0.0
Transition	0.00	0.0

Largest Single Issuance	
Issue Year	2021
Issuer	BIM Land
Size (USD)	200 million
Currency	USD
Label	Green
Tenor	5

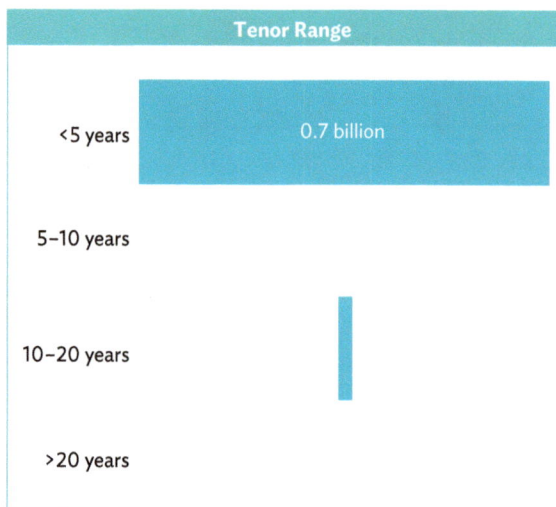

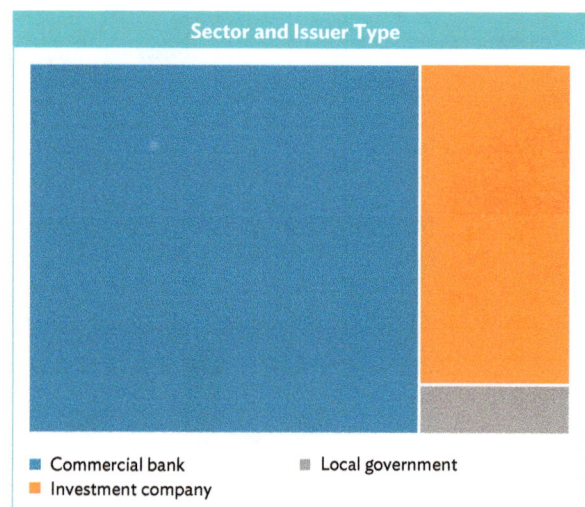

Tenor Range

<5 years	0.7 billion
5–10 years	
10–20 years	
>20 years	

Sector and Issuer Type

- Commercial bank
- Investment company
- Local government

COVID-19 = coronavirus disease, VND = Vietnamese dong, USD = United States dollar.
Source: Climate Bonds Initiative.

APPENDIX 2
Policy Summaries
for Indonesia, Malaysia, the Philippines, Singapore, Thailand, and Viet Nam

Economy	Policy	Date	Lead Organization	Description	Link
Indonesia	Roadmap for Sustainable Finance in Indonesia	2015–2019	Indonesia's Financial Services Authority (OJK)	Explains targeted conditions about sustainable finance in Indonesia for the medium-term period (2015–2019) and long-term period (2015–2024) aim of achieving sustainable development through the comprehensive support of the financial service industry.	Source
Indonesia	Regulation on the Issuance and Terms of Green Bonds	2017	OJK	The regulation sets standards for green bond issuance. It is a follow up to the sustainable finance roadmap and requires all financial service institutions to set out a sustainable finance action plan.	Source
Indonesia	OJK Regulation No. 60/2017 on Green Bonds	2017	OJK	The regulation establishes the basic guideline and requirements for a green bond issuance, mainly on the green requirements on the use of proceeds. There are no cost incentives for green bond issuance in this regulation yet.	Source
Indonesia	Technical Guidelines for Banks on the Implementation of OJK Regulation	2018	OJK	The guidelines provide general guidelines on the definition of sustainable business activities and sustainable finance criteria for conventional banks.	Source
Indonesia	Regulation of Implementation Sustainable Finance for Financial Institution	2017	OJK	The regulation sets obligations and requirements in implementing sustainable finance for financial institutions, issuers and public companies. It is a follow up to the sustainable finance roadmap and requires all financial service institutions to set out a sustainable finance action plan.	Source

continued on next page

Table continued

Economy	Policy	Date	Lead Organization	Description	Link
Indonesia	Sustainable Finance Roadmap Phase II	2020–2024	OJK	The roadmap accelerates the implementation of environmental, social, and governance aspects in Indonesia. Phase II focuses on creating a comprehensive sustainable finance ecosystem that involves all related parties and promoting cooperation at various levels.	Source
Indonesia	National Strategy for Financial Market Development	2018–2024	The Ministry of Finance, Bank Indonesia, and OJK	The strategy is a single policy framework oriented toward creating deep, liquid, efficient, inclusive, and secure financial markets, including the thematic bond market.	Source
Indonesia	Indonesian Financial Services Sector Master Plan	2021–2025	OJK	The plan aids the recovery of the national economy and enhances the financial service sector resiliency and competitiveness.	Source
Indonesia	OJK Circular Letter 16/SEOJK.04/2021	2021	OJK	The circular extends the scope of the annual reporting requirements (in OJK regulation No. 29/2016) to include a sustainable reporting component. This circular letter sets out the content and component of a sustainability report. All issuer and public companies are required to implement sustainable finance by 2021 and to submit sustainability reporting by 2022.	Source
Indonesia	Technical Guidelines for Securities Companies on the Implementation of OJK Sustainable Finance Regulation	2021	OJK	This provides general guidelines on the principles of sustainable finance for securities companies, specifically for underwriters and broker-dealer firms. Guidelines for wealth management firms will be launched separately.	Source
Indonesia	Indonesia Green Taxonomy Edition 1.0	2022	OJK	The taxonomy outlines green standards and establishes a national taxonomy as the basis for sustainable business and investment. The taxonomy will make it easier for business actors to improve the quality of risk management.	Source
Malaysia	Sustainable and Responsible Investment (SRI) Sukuk Framework	2014	Securities Commission Malaysia	The SRI Sukuk Framework was first launched in 2014 to facilitate the creation of an ecosystem that promotes sustainable and responsible investing for SRI investors and issuers. SRI *sukuk* is where the *sukuk* proceeds will be applied exclusively for funding of any activities or transactions relating to the eligible SRI projects.	Source

continued on next page

Table continued

Economy	Policy	Date	Lead Organization	Description	Link
Malaysia	SRI Sukuk and Bond Grant Scheme	2018	Securities Commission Malaysia	Launched as the Green SRI Sukuk Grant Scheme in 2018, the grant was expanded and renamed as the SRI Sukuk and Bond Grant Scheme in 2021 and is now applicable to all *sukuk* issued under the SRI Sukuk Framework or bonds issued under the ASEAN Green, Social, and Sustainability Bond Standards. Eligible issuers can claim the grant to offset up to 90% of the external review costs incurred, subject to a maximum of MYR300,000 per issuance.	Source
Malaysia	SRI Roadmap for the Malaysian Capital Market	2019	Securities Commission Malaysia	The SRI roadmap aims to create a facilitative SRI ecosystem and chart the role of the capital market in driving Malaysia's sustainable development.	Source
The Philippines	Roadmap on Local Currency Debt Market Development	2017	Bangko Sentral ng Pilipinas (BSP), Bureau of the Treasury, and the Securities and Exchange Commission	The roadmap aims to broaden and deepen the financial sector and support debt management in the country.	Source
The Philippines	Inter-Agency Task Force on Green Finance	2019	Department of Finance, BSP	The task force harmonizes existing sustainability policies by identifying policy or technical gaps then allocating the appropriate resources to address these gaps.	Source
The Philippines	Sustainable Finance Framework	2020	BSP	The framework calls for the integration of sustainability into banks' operations, including disclosure requirements and environmental and social risk management systems.	Source
The Philippines	Sustainable Finance Guiding Principles	2021	Green Inter-Agency (Inter-Agency Technical Working Group for Sustainable Finance)	These are principles-based guidance identifying economic activities that contribute to supporting sustainable development, with a focus on addressing the impacts of climate change and encouraging the flow of capital to these activities.	Source
The Philippines	Philippine Sustainable Finance Roadmap	2021	Inter-Agency Technical Working Group for Sustainable Finance	The roadmap coordinates and harmonizes the government's green policies including outlines government actions in pursuit of developing a sustainable finance ecosystem.[a]	Source
The Philippines	Environmental and Social Risk Management Framework	2021	BSP	The framework govern the integration of environmental and social risks in the enterprise-wide risk management frameworks of banks and institutionalize the adoption of sustainability principles.	Source

continued on next page

Table continued

Economy	Policy	Date	Lead Organization	Description	Link
Singapore	Green Bond Grant Scheme	2017	Monetary Authority of Singapore (MAS)	This scheme encourages the issuance of green bonds (superseded by the Sustainable Bond Grant Scheme in 2019).	Source
Singapore	Sustainable Bond Grant Scheme	2019	MAS	This scheme encourages the issuance of green, social, and sustainability bonds.	Source
Singapore	Green Finance Action Plan	2019	MAS	This plan strengthens the financial sector's resilience to environmental risks, develops green financial solutions, enhances comparability and reliability of sustainability-related disclosures, builds knowledge and capabilities in sustainable finance, and leverages innovation and technology.	Source
Singapore	Guidelines on Environmental Risk Management for Banks	2020	MAS	These guidelines assess how financial institutions incorporate environmental risk management into business operations.	Source
Singapore	Singapore Green Plan 2030	2021	Government of Singapore	The plan advances Singapore's national agenda on sustainable development.	Source
Thailand	Sustainability Development Roadmap	2013-2015, 2019	The Securities and Exchange Commission	The Securities and Exchange Commission (SEC) started to focus on sustainability, notably connecting the topics of corporate governance, ESG, sustainability, and anticorruption in the Sustainability Development Roadmap which was adopted as part of the SEC Strategic Plan, 2013–2015. The roadmap was drafted in 2019, companies are recommended to focus on corporate governance in substance for creating sustainable growth and corporate social responsibility in the process as a driving force of its value chain.	Source
Thailand	Sustainable Banking Guidelines	2019	Thai Bankers' Association	Issued as guidance for banks to establish a responsible lending strategy to manage their environmental and social impacts and risks	Source
Thailand	Green, Social, and Sustainability Bond Guidelines	2019	The Securities and Exchange Commission	The guidelines promote the issuance and offer for sale of green bonds, social bonds, and sustainability bonds requiring issuers to align with the ASEAN Green, Social, and Sustainability Bond Standards, ICMA principles, or any internationally accepted standards or guidelines.	Source

continued on next page

Table continued

Economy	Policy	Date	Lead Organization	Description	Link
Thailand	Strategic Plan 2020–2022	2020	The Securities and Exchange Commission	This plan has incorporated Sustainability Development Roadmap to develop an ecosystem for sustainable finance through (i) emphasizing the benefits of ESG integration in business operation as well as ESG risks to issuers; (ii) creating investors' awareness of ESG issues that will consequently affect business performance and return on investment by ensuring availability of disclosure standards, reliable assessors, and sources of ESG-related information for investment decision-making; and (iii) laying out a blueprint as a driving force with clear direction.	Source
Thailand	Sustainability-Linked Bond Regulations and Guidelines	2021	The Securities and Exchange Commission	These promote the issuance and offer for sale of sustainability-linked bonds; the regulations and guidelines are based on internationally accepted standards and incorporate references to conventional debt securities regulations.	English version not available
Thailand	Sustainable Finance Initiatives for Thailand	2021	Working Group on Sustainable Finance	Key strategic initiative include developing a practical taxonomy and implementing effective incentives.	Source
Viet Nam	Bond Market Development Roadmap	2017–2020	Government of Viet Nam	The roadmap set out specific goals to improve the domestic bond market during its coverage period.	Source
Viet Nam	Green Growth Strategy	2011–2020	Government of Viet Nam	This strategy paved the way for green finance to grow in Viet Nam.	Source
Viet Nam	Decree No. 153/2020/ND-CP: Private placement of corporate bonds and trading of privately placed corporate bonds in the domestic market and offering of corporate bonds to the international market	2020	Government of Viet Nam	The decree established guidelines on the placement and trading of both conventional and green bonds in the onshore and offshore markets.	Source
Viet Nam	Environmental Protection Law	2020	National Assembly of Viet Nam	Definitions and general requirements of green bonds and potential incentives applicable to eligible issuers were included in this law.	Source

[a] S&P Global Market Intelligence. 2022. Using ESG Analysis to Support a Sustainable Future. 19 January. https://www.spglobal.com/marketintelligence/en/news-insights/blog/using-esg-analysis-to-support-a-sustainable-future.